Eric Hobsbawm was born in  cated in Austria, Germany and I British Academy and of the Am Sciences, and a Foreign Member honorary degrees from universities in several countries. He taught until retirement at Birkbeck College, University of London, and then at the New School for Social Research in New York. In addition to *The Age of Revolution*, *The Age of Capital*, *The Age of Empire* and *The Age of Extremes*, his books include *Bandits*, *Revolutionaries*, *Uncommon People* and his memoir, *Interesting Times*.

Praise for *Globalisation, Democracy and Terrorism*

'This collection of recent essays gives a good sense of the vigour and passion with which this famous intellectual surveys the contemporary world'
Sunday Telegraph

'Britain's greatest living left-wing historian . . . *Globalisation, Democracy and Terrorism* picks up where the bestselling *The Age of Extremes* and *The New Century* left off'
The Scotsman

'Eric Hobsbawm rounds off his splendid histories of the nineteenth and twentieth centuries with a look at the factors that will shape the twenty-first . . . This book contains many valuable insights, presented in a clear and concrete fashion; it deserves to be widely read'
Socialist Review

'The lasting impression of these speeches is of a fiercely unsentimental historian who has not stopped speaking out against Western imperialism'
Metro

Globalisation, Democracy and Terrorism

Eric Hobsbawm

ABACUS

First published in Great Britain in 2007 by Little, Brown
This paperback edition published in 2008 by Abacus
Reprinted 2008

A CIP catalogue record for this book
is available from the British Library.

ISBN 978-0-349-12066-9

Typeset in Baskerville by M Rules
Printed and bound in Great Britain by
Clays Ltd, St Ives plc

Papers used by Abacus are natural, renewable and recyclable
products made from wood grown in sustainable forests and certified
in accordance with the rules of the Forest Stewardship Council.

Mixed Sources
Product group from well-managed
forests and other controlled sources
www.fsc.org Cert no. SGS-COC-004081
© 1996 Forest Stewardship Council
FSC

Abacus
An imprint of
Little, Brown Book Group
100 Victoria Embankment
London EC4Y 0DY

An Hachette Livre UK Company
www.hachettelivre.co.uk

www.littlebrown.co.uk

To Birkbeck

Contents

Preface

The twentieth century was the most extraordinary era in the history of humanity, combining as it did unparalleled human catastrophes, substantial material improvement and an unprecedented increase in our capacity to transform, and perhaps to destroy, the face of our planet – and even to penetrate outside it. How are we to look back on that 'age of extremes', or forward at the prospects for the new era which has emerged from the old? The present collection of essays is a historian's attempt to survey, analyse and understand the situation of the world at the start of the third millennium, and some of the main political problems confronting us today. They supplement and bring up to date what I have written in earlier publications, notably my history of the 'short twentieth century', *The Age of Extremes*, a conversation on *The New Century* with Antonio Polito, and *Nations and Nationalism*. Such attempts are necessary. What can historians contribute to this task? Their main function,

1

apart from remembering what others have forgotten, or wish to forget, is to stand back, so far as possible, from the contemporary record and see it in a broader context and in a longer perspective.

In this collection of studies, mainly on political themes, I have chosen to focus on five areas which require clear and informed thinking today: the general question of war and peace in the twenty-first century; the past and future of world empires; the nature and the changing context of nationalism; the prospects of liberal democracy; and the question of political violence and terror. All take place on a world scene dominated by two linked developments: the enormous and continuing acceleration of the ability of the human species to change the planet by means of technology and economic activity, and globalisation. The first of these, unfortunately, has so far had no significant impact on those who make political decisions. Maximising economic growth remains the aim of governments, nor is there a realistic prospect of any effective steps to meet the crisis of global warming. On the other hand, since the 1960s the accelerating advance of globalisation, that is to say the world as a single unit of interconnected activities unhampered by local boundaries, has had a profound political and cultural impact, especially in its currently dominant form of an uncontrolled global free market. It is not specifically discussed in these essays, chiefly because politics is the one field of human activity that remains practically unaffected by it. In their attempt at the dubious task of quantifying it, the Swiss KOF Index of Globalisation (2007) has had no difficulty in finding indices of economic and information

2

flows, personal contacts or cultural diffusion – for example, the number of McDonald's restaurants and IKEAs per capita – but it can think of no better measures for 'political globalisation' than the number of embassies in a country, its membership of international organisations, and its participation in UN Security Council missions.

A general discussion of globalisation may be outside the range of this book, but three general observations about it are particularly relevant to its themes.

First, the currently fashionable free-market globalisation has brought about a dramatic growth in economic and social inequalities both within states and internationally. There is no sign that this polarisation is not continuing within countries, in spite of a general diminution of extreme poverty. This surge of inequality, especially in the conditions of extreme economic instability such as those created by the global free market in the 1990s, is at the root of the major social and political tensions of the new century. Insofar as international inequalities may be under pressure from the rise of the new Asian economies, both the threat to the relatively astronomic standards of living of the peoples of the old North, and the practical impossibility of achieving anything like it for the vast populations of such countries as India and China, will produce its own domestic and international tensions.

Second, the impact of this globalisation is felt most by those who benefit from it least. Hence the growing polarisation of views about it, between those who are potentially sheltered from its negative effects – the entrepreneurs who can 'out-source' their costs to countries of cheap labour, the high-tech professionals and graduates of higher education who can get work in any high-income market economy – and those who are not. That is why for most of those who live by the wages or salaries of their employment in the old 'developed countries' the early twenty-first century offers a troubling, not to say sinister, prospect. The global free market has undermined the ability of their states and welfare systems to protect their way of life. In a global economy they compete with men and women abroad, of equal qualifications but paid a fraction of the Western pay-packet; and at home it is under pressure from the globalisation of what Marx called 'the reserve army of labour' of immigrants from the villages of the great global zones of poverty. Situations such as this do not promise an era of political and social stability.

Third, while the actual scale of globalisation remains modest, except perhaps in a number of generally smallish states, mainly in Europe, its political and cultural impact is disproportionately large. Thus immigration is a major political problem in most developed economies of the West, even though the world share of humans living in a country other than the one in which they were born is no more than 3 per cent. In the 2007 KOF index of economic globalisation, the US is in 39th place, Germany in 40th, China in 55th, Brazil in 60th, South Korea in 62nd, Japan in 67th and India in 105th, though all except Brazil are somewhat higher in the ranking of 'social globalisation' (the UK is the only major economy in the top ten of both economic and social globalisation).* While

*The rankings are based on the data for 2004.

this may or may not be a historically temporary phenomenon, in the short term this disproportionately large impact may well have serious national and international political consequences. I would guess that, in one way or another, political resistance, though unlikely to revive formal protectionist policies, is likely to slow down the progress of free-market globalisation in the next decade or two.

I hope that the chapters on war, hegemony, empires and imperialism, the current state of nationalism, and the transformations of public violence and terror make sense to the reader without further comment from their author. So, I hope, do the two chapters on democracy, although the author is aware that it is highly controversial to try to show that one of the most sacred cows of vulgar Western political discourse yields less milk than is usually supposed. More nonsense and meaningless blather is talked in Western public discourse today about democracy, and specifically about the miraculous qualities assigned to governments elected by arithmetical majorities of voters choosing between rival parties, than about almost any other word or political concept. In recent US rhetoric the word has lost all contact with reality. My chapters are a small contribution to the necessary task of cooling hot air through the application of reason and common sense, while remaining firmly committed to government for the people – all the people, rich and poor, stupid and clever, informed and ignorant – and with their consultation and consent.

The pieces collected here and updated where necessary, mostly delivered as lectures before various audiences, try to set out and explain the situation in which the world, or large parts of it, finds itself today. They may help to define the problems we confront at the start of the new century, but they do not propose programmes or practical solutions. They were written between 2000 and 2006 and therefore reflect the specific international concerns of this period, which was dominated by the decision of the US government in 2001 to assert a single-handed world hegemony, denouncing hitherto accepted international conventions, reserving its right to launch wars of aggression or other military operations whenever it wanted to, and actually doing so. Given the debacle of the Iraq War, it is no longer necessary to demonstrate that this project was unrealistic, and the question would we have wanted it to succeed or not is therefore entirely academic. Nevertheless, it should be evident, and readers should bear in mind, that my essays were written by an author who is deeply critical of the project. This is partly because of the strength and indestructibility of the author's political convictions, including a hostility to imperialism, whether of great powers which claim they are doing their victims a favour by conquering them, or of white men assuming automatic superiority for themselves and their arrangements to those of other skin colours. It is also due to a rationally justifiable suspicion of the megalomania that is the occupational disease of states and rulers who believe there are no limits on their power or success.

Most of the arguments and lies justifying US actions since 2001 by US and British politicians, paid or unpaid advocates, rhetoricians, press agents, lobbyists and amateur ideologists no longer need detain us. However, a less disreputable case has been made, not for the Iraq War but for the general proposition that armed cross-border intervention to preserve or establish human rights is legitimate and sometimes necessary in an era of growing global barbarity, violence and disorder. For some, this implies the desirability of a world imperial hegemony, and specifically one exercised by the only power capable of establishing it, the US. This proposition, which may be called the imperialism of human rights, entered public debate in the course of the Balkan conflicts arising out of the disintegration of Communist Yugoslavia, especially in Bosnia, which seemed to suggest that only outside armed force could put an end to endless mutual massacre and that only the US was able and willing to use such force. That the US had no particular interests, historic, political or economic, in the region made its intervention more impressive and apparently selfless. I have taken note of it in my essays. Though my essays, especially 'Spreading Democracy', contain reasons for rejecting it, some additional observations on this position may not be out of place.

It is fundamentally flawed by the fact that great powers in the pursuit of their international policies may do things that suit the champions of human rights, and be aware of the publicity value of doing so, but this is quite incidental to their purposes, which, if they think it necessary, are today pursued with the ruthless barbarism that is the heritage of the twentieth century. The relationship of those for whom a great human cause is central with any state can be one of ad hoc alliance or opposition, but never of permanent identification. Even the rare case of young revolutionary states genuinely seeking to spread their universal message – France after 1792, Russia after 1917, but not, as it happens, George Washington's isolationist USA – is always short-lived. The default position of any state is to pursue its interests.

Beyond this, the humanitarian case for armed intervention in the affairs of states rests on three assumptions: that intolerable situations may arise in the contemporary world – usually massacre, or even genocide – which call for it; that no other ways of dealing with them are possible; and that the benefits of doing so are patently greater than the costs. All these assumptions are sometimes justified, although, as the debate on Iraq and Iran proves, there is rarely universal agreement about what precisely constitutes an 'intolerable situation'. Probably there was consensus in the two most obvious cases of justified intervention: the invasion of Kampuchea by Vietnam, which put an end to the appalling regime of Pol Pot's 'killing fields' (1978), and the destruction of Idi Amin's regime of terror in Uganda by Tanzania (1979). (Of course, not all rapid and successful foreign armed interventions in local crisis situations have produced such satisfactory results – for more doubtful examples, consider Liberia, East Timor.) Both were achieved by brief incursions and produced immediate benefits and probably some lasting improvements, while implying no systematic abrogation of the established principle of non-interference in the internal affairs of sovereign states. Incidentally, they had no imperial implications, nor did they involve wider world politics. Indeed, both the US and China continued to support the deposed Pol Pot. Such ad hoc interventions are irrelevant to the case for the desirability of a world hegemony by the US.

This is not the case for the armed interventions of recent years, which have, in any case, been selective, not touching what by humanitarian standards were some of the very worst cases of atrocity, notably the central African genocide. In the Balkans of the 1990s humanitarian concern was certainly a significant factor, though not the only one. Probably, though the opposite has been argued, in Bosnia outside intervention helped to end the local bloodshed earlier than if the war between Serbs, Croats and Bosnian Muslims had been allowed to continue to its conclusion, but the region remains unsettled. It is by no means clear whether in 1999 armed intervention was the only way to settle the problems raised by a rebellion against Serbia of an extremist minority group among Albanian nationalists in Kosovo, or indeed, whether it was the threat of invasion rather than Russian diplomacy that ended Serbian intransigence. Its humanitarian basis was rather more doubtful than in Bosnia, and by provoking Serbia into the mass expulsion of the Kosovo Albanians, as well as the civilian casualties of the war itself and some months of destructive bombing of Serbia, it may actually have made the humanitarian situation worse. Nor have relations between Serbs and Albanians been stabilised. However, at least the Balkan interventions were rapid, and in the short run decisive, though so far nobody, except perhaps Croatia, has reason to feel satisfied with the outcome.

On the other hand, the wars in Afghanistan and Iraq since 2001 were US military operations not undertaken for humanitarian reasons, though justified to humanitarian public opinion on the ground that they removed some rather unsavoury regimes. But for 9/11, not even the US would have regarded the situation in either country as calling for immediate invasion. Afghanistan was accepted by other states on old-fashioned 'realist' grounds, Iraq was almost universally condemned. Though the Taliban and Saddam Hussein's regimes were rapidly overthrown, neither war achieved victory, and certainly not the aims announced at the outset: the establishment of democratic regimes in line with Western values, a beacon to other as yet undemocratised societies in the region. Both, but especially the catastrophic Iraq War, proved to be lengthy, massively destructive and bloody, and still continue at the time of writing without a prospect of conclusion.

In all these cases, armed intervention has come from foreign states with far superior military power and resources. In none of them has it so far produced stable solutions. In all the countries concerned, foreign military occupation and political supervision continue. In the best of cases, but plainly not in Afghanistan and Iraq, intervention has ended bloody wars and produced some kind of peace, but the positive results, as in the Balkans, are disappointing. In the worst of cases, Iraq, nobody would seriously deny that the situation of the people whose liberation was the official excuse for the war, is worse than before. The recent record of armed interventions in the affairs of other countries, even by superpowers, is not one of success.

This failure is based partly on an assumption that also lies behind much of the imperialism of human rights, that regimes of barbarity and tyranny are immune to internal change, so that only outside force can bring about their end and the consequent diffusion of our values and political or legal institutions. These assumptions are inherited from the days when Cold Warriors denounced 'totalitarianism'. They should not have survived the end of the USSR, or, for that matter, the evident process of internal democratisation after 1980 in several once unsavoury non-communist authoritarian, militarist and dictatorial regimes in Asia and South America. They are also based on the belief that acts of force can instantly bring about major cultural transformations. But this is not so. The diffusion of values and institutions can hardly ever be brought about by a sudden imposition by outside force, unless conditions are already present locally which make them adaptable and their introduction acceptable. Democracy and Western values and human rights are not like some technological importations whose benefits are immediately obvious and will be adopted in the same manner by all who can use them and afford them, like the peaceful bicycle and the murderous AK47, or technical services like airports. If they were, there would be more political similarity between the numerous states of Europe, Asia and Africa all living (in theory) under similar democratic constitutions. In a word, there are very few shortcuts in history – a lesson the author has learned, not least from living through and reflecting on much of the past century.

Finally, a word of thanks to those who provided the occasion for the first presentation of these studies. Chapter 1 is based on a paper written for the colloquium to commemorate the Centenary of the Nobel Peace Prize (Oslo, 2001), chapter 2 on the Nikhil Chakravarty Memorial Lecture in Delhi, 2004, by invitation of the *Indian Review of Books*; chapter 3 was delivered as a Massey Lecture at Harvard University in 2005, chapter 4 as an inaugural address at the presentation of an honorary degree at the University of Thessaloniki, Greece, in 2004. Chapter 5 is a considerable elaboration of a preface written for a new edition of the German edition of *Nations and Nationalism* (Campus Verlag, Frankfurt, 2004). Chapter 6 was originally given and printed as an Athenaeum Lecture at that club in 2000. Chapter 7 was published as a contribution to an issue of *Foreign Policy* devoted to 'the world's most dangerous ideas' (September/ October 2004); chapter 8 had its remote starting point in some notes for a seminar paper on the subject of terror at Columbia University, New York, in the early 1990s; chapter 9 was given at Birkbeck College as a public lecture, part of a series on 'Violence', in 2006; and chapter 10 was written for and published by *Le Monde Diplomatique* in 2003. I would also like to thank the colleagues and others who took trouble to listen to me and to discuss my presentations, notably in New Delhi, Harvard and New York. As a professional author I am obliged to my Italian publishers who first suggested that a collection of pieces such as this had sufficient coherence to form a short book worth publishing, and to Bruce Hunter and Ania Corless who persuaded both me and other publishers.

On the other hand I ought to apologise for the elements of inevitable duplication in a book based on a number of lectures and talks given on separate occasions. I have eliminated some, but to have eliminated them all would have damaged the continuity of argument in each chapter – and perhaps the sense that the book forms a coherent whole. Perhaps they may also help to loosen the fairly concentrated argument of some chapters. Besides, a modicum of repetition is part of the toolkit of an author who cannot get out of the lifetime habit of wanting to teach, that is, to persuade as well as to expound. I hope I have not exceeded that modicum.

E. J. Hobsbawm, London, 2007

1

War and Peace in the Twentieth Century

The twentieth century was the most murderous in recorded history. The total number of deaths caused by or associated with its wars has been estimated at 187 million, the equivalent of more than 10 per cent of the world's population in 1913.[1] Taken as having begun in 1914, it has been a century of almost unbroken war, with few and brief periods without organised armed conflict somewhere. It was dominated by world wars: that is to say, by wars between territorial states or alliances of states. The period from 1914 to 1945 can be regarded as a single 'Thirty Years War' interrupted only by a pause in the 1920s, between the final withdrawal of the Japanese from the Soviet Far East in 1922 and the beginning of the Japanese attack on Manchuria in 1931. This was followed, almost immediately, by some forty years of Cold War, which conformed to the great philosopher Thomas Hobbes's definition of war as consisting 'not in battle only or the act of fighting, but in a tract of time wherein the will to contend by battle is sufficiently known'. It is a matter for debate how far the actions in which US armed forces have been involved since the end of the Cold War in various parts of the globe constitute a continuation of the era of world war. There can be no doubt, however, that the 1990s were filled with formal and informal military conflict, in Europe, Africa and western and central Asia. The world as a whole has not been at peace since 1914, and it is not at peace now.

Nevertheless, the century cannot be treated as a single block, either chronologically or geographically. Chronologically, it falls into three periods: the era of world war centred on Germany (1914 to 1945), the era of confrontation between the two superpowers (1945 to 1989), and the era since the end of the classic international power system. I shall call these periods I, II and III. Geographically, the impact of military operations has been highly unequal. With one exception (the Chaco War of 1932–5) there were no significant inter-state wars, as distinct from civil wars, in the western hemisphere (the Americas) in the twentieth century. Enemy military operations have barely touched these territories – hence the shock of the bombing of the World Trade Center and the Pentagon on 11 September 2001. Since 1945, inter-state wars have also disappeared from Europe, which had until then been the main battlefield region. Although in period III war returned to south-east Europe, it seems very unlikely to recur in the rest of the continent. On the other hand, during period II inter-state wars, not necessarily unconnected with the global confrontation, remained endemic in the Middle East and south Asia, and major wars directly springing from the global confrontation occurred in east and south-east Asia (Korea, Indochina). At the same time, areas such as sub-Saharan Africa, which had been comparatively unaffected by war in period I (apart from Ethiopia, belatedly subject to colonial conquest by Italy in 1935–6), came to be theatres of armed conflict during period II, and witnessed major scenes of carnage and suffering in period III.

Two other characteristics of war in the twentieth century stand out, the first less obviously than the second. At the start of the twenty-first century we find ourselves in a world where armed operations are no longer essentially in the hands of governments or their authorised agents, and where the contending parties have no common characteristics, status or objectives, except the willingness to use violence. Inter-state wars dominated the image of war so much in periods I and II that civil wars or other armed conflicts within the territories of existing states or empires were somewhat obscured. Even the civil wars in the territories of the Russian empire after the October Revolution, and those which took place after the collapse of the Chinese empire, could be fitted into the framework of international conflicts, insofar as they were inseparable from them. On the other hand, Latin America may not have seen armies crossing state frontiers in the twentieth century, but it has been the scene of major civil conflicts: in Mexico after 1911, for instance, in Colombia since 1948, and in various Central American countries during period II. It is not generally recognised that the number of international wars has declined fairly continuously since the mid-1960s, when internal conflicts became more common

17

than those fought between states. The number of conflicts within state frontiers continued to rise steeply until it levelled off in the 1990s.[2]

More familiar is the erosion of the distinction between combatants and non-combatants. The two world wars of the first half of the century involved the entire populations of belligerent countries; both combatants and non-combatants suffered. In the course of the century, however, the burden of war shifted increasingly from armed forces to civilians, who were not only its victims, but increasingly the object of military or military-political operations. The contrast between the First World War and the Second is dramatic: only 5 per cent of those who died in the former conflict were civilians; in the latter, that figure increased to 66 per cent. It is generally supposed that 80 to 90 per cent of those affected by war today are civilians. The proportion has increased since the end of the Cold War because most military operations since then have been conducted not by conscript armies, but by quite small bodies of regular or irregular troops, in many cases operating high-technology weapons and protected against the risk of incurring casualties. While it is true that high-tech weaponry has made it possible in some cases to re-establish a distinction between military and civilian targets, and therefore between combatants and non-combatants, there is no reason to doubt that the main victims of wars will continue to be civilians.

What is more, the suffering of civilians is not proportionate to the scale or intensity of military operations. In strictly military terms, the two-week war between India and Pakistan over the independence of Bangladesh in 1971 was a modest affair, but it produced ten million refugees. The fighting between armed units in Africa during the 1990s can hardly have involved more than a few thousand mostly ill-armed combatants, yet it produced, at its peak, almost seven million refugees – a far greater number than at any time during the Cold War, when the continent had been the scene of proxy wars between the superpowers.[3]

This phenomenon is not confined to poor and remote areas. In some ways the effect of war on civilian life is magnified by globalisation and the world's increasing reliance on a constant, unbroken flow of communications, technical services, deliveries and supplies. Even a comparatively brief interruption of this flow – for instance, the few days' closure of US airspace after 9/11 – can have considerable, perhaps lasting effects on the global economy.

It would be easier to write about the subject of war and peace in the twentieth century if the difference between the two remained as clear-cut as it was supposed to be at the beginning of the century, in the days when the Hague Conventions of 1899 and 1907 codified the rules of war. Conflicts were supposed to take place primarily between sovereign states or, if they occurred within the territory of one particular state, between parties sufficiently organised to be accorded belligerent status by other sovereign states. War was supposed to be sharply distinguished from peace, by a declaration of war at one end and a treaty of peace at the other. Military operations were supposed to distinguish clearly between combatants – marked as such by the uniforms they wore, or by other signs of belonging to an organised armed force – and non-combatant civilians.

War was supposed to be between combatants. Non-combatants should, so far as possible, be protected in wartime. It was always understood that these conventions did not cover all civil and international armed conflicts, and notably not those arising out of the imperial expansion of Western states in regions not under the jurisdiction of internationally recognised sovereign states, even though some (but by no means all) of these conflicts were known as 'wars'. Nor did they cover large rebellions against established states, such as the so-called Indian Mutiny; nor the recurrent armed activity in regions beyond the effective control of the states or imperial authorities nominally ruling them, such as the raiding and blood-feuding in the mountains of Afghanistan or Morocco. Nevertheless, the Hague Conventions still served as guidelines in the First World War. In the course of the twentieth century, this relative clarity was replaced by confusion.

First, the line between inter-state conflicts and conflicts within states – that is, between international and civil wars – became hazy, because the twentieth century was characteristically a century not only of wars, but also of revolutions and the break-up of empires. Revolutions or liberation struggles within a state had implications for the international situation, particularly during the Cold War. Conversely, after the Russian Revolution, intervention by states in the internal affairs of other states of which they disapproved became common, at least where it seemed comparatively risk-free. This remains the case.

Second, the clear distinction between war and peace became obscure. Except for here and there, the Second World War neither began with declarations of war nor ended with treaties of peace. It was followed by a period so hard to classify as either war or peace in the old sense that the neologism 'Cold War' had to be invented to describe it. The sheer obscurity of the position since the Cold War is illustrated by the current state of affairs in the Middle East. Before the Iraq War neither 'peace' nor 'war' correctly described the situation in Iraq since the formal end of the Gulf War – the country was still bombed almost daily by foreign powers. Nor is either term fully applicable to the relations between Palestinians and Israelis, or those between Israel and its neighbours Lebanon and Syria. All this is an unfortunate legacy of the twentieth-century world wars, but also of war's increasingly powerful machinery of mass propaganda, and of a period of confrontation between incompatible and passion-laden ideologies which brought into wars a crusading element comparable to that seen in religious conflicts of the past. These conflicts, unlike the traditional wars of the international power system, were increasingly waged for non-negotiable ends such as 'unconditional surrender'. Since both wars and victories were seen as total, any limitation on a belligerent's capacity to win that might be imposed by the accepted conventions of eighteenth- and nineteenth-century warfare, even formal declarations of war, was rejected. So was any limitation on the victor's power to assert its will. Experience had shown that agreements reached in peace treaties could easily be broken.

In recent years, the situation has been further complicated by the tendency in public rhetoric for the term 'war' to be used to refer to the deployment of organised force against various national or international activities regarded as anti-social – 'the war against the Mafia', for example, or 'the war against the drug cartels'. Not only is the fight to control, or even to eliminate, such organisations or networks, including small-scale terrorist groups, quite different from the major operations of war; it also confuses the actions of two types of armed force. One – let us call them 'soldiers' – is directed against other armed forces with the object of defeating them. The action of the other – let us call them 'police' – sets out to maintain or re-establish the required degree of law and public order within an existing political entity, typically a state. Victory, which has no necessary moral connotation, is the object of one force; the bringing to justice of offenders against the law, which does have a moral connotation, is the object of the other.

Such a distinction is easier to draw in theory than in practice, however. Homicide by a soldier in battle is not in itself a breach of the law, unlike homicide in all functioning territorial states. But what if a member of the IRA regards himself as a belligerent, even though official UK law regards him as a murderer? Were the operations in Northern Ireland a war, as the IRA held them to be, or an attempt in the face of law-breakers to maintain orderly government in one province of the United Kingdom? Since not only a formidable local police force but a national army was mobilised against the IRA for thirty years or so, we may conclude that it was a war, but one systematically run like a police operation, in a way that minimised casualties and the disruption of life in the province. In the end, there was a negotiated settlement – one which, typically, has not so far brought peace, merely an extended absence of fighting. Such are the complexities and confusions of the relations between peace and war at the start of the new century. They are well illustrated by the military and other operations in which the US and its allies are at present engaged.

There is now, as there was throughout the twentieth century, a complete absence of any effective global authority capable of controlling or settling armed disputes. Globalisation has advanced in almost every respect – economically, technologically, culturally, even linguistically – except one: politically and militarily, territorial states remain the only effective authorities. There are officially about two hundred states, but in practice only a handful count, of which the US is overwhelmingly the most powerful. However, no state or empire has ever been large, rich or powerful enough to maintain hegemony over the political world, let alone to establish political and military supremacy over the globe. The world is too big, complicated and plural. There is no likelihood that the US, or any other conceivable single state power, could establish lasting control, even if it wanted to.

A single superpower cannot compensate for the absence of global authorities, especially given the lack of conventions – relating to international disarmament, for instance, or weapons control – strong enough to be voluntarily accepted as binding by major states. Some such authorities exist, notably the United Nations, various technical and financial bodies such as the International Monetary Fund, the World Bank and the World Trade Organisation, and some international tribunals. But none has any effective power other than that granted to them by agreements between states, or thanks to the backing of powerful states, or voluntarily accepted by states. Regrettable as this may be, it is not likely to change in the foreseeable future.

Since only states wield real power, the risk is that international institutions will be ineffective or lack universal legitimacy when they try to deal with offences such as war crimes.[4] Even when world courts are established by general agreement (for example, the International Criminal Court set up by the UN Rome Statute of 17 July 1998), their judgments will not necessarily be accepted as legitimate and binding, so long as powerful states are in a position to disregard them. A consortium of powerful states may be strong enough to ensure that some offenders from weaker states are brought before these tribunals, perhaps curbing the cruelty of armed conflict in certain areas. This is an example, however, of the traditional exercise of power and influence within an international state system, not of the exercise of international law.*

There is, however, a major difference between the twenty-first and twentieth centuries: the idea that war takes place in a world divided into territorial areas under the authority of effective governments which possess a monopoly of the means of public power and coercion has ceased to apply. It was never applicable to countries experiencing revolution, or to the fragments of disintegrated empires, but until recently most new revolutionary or

---

*This is also the case, by definition, where individual states accept international humanitarian law and unilaterally assert the right to apply it to the citizens of other countries in their national tribunals – as, notably, the Spanish courts, supported by the British House of Lords, did in the case of General Pinochet.

post-colonial regimes – China between 1911 and 1949 is the main exception – emerged fairly quickly as more or less organised and functioning successor regimes and states.

Over the past thirty years or so, however, the territorial state has, for various reasons, lost its traditional monopoly of armed force, much of its former stability and power, and, increasingly, the fundamental sense of legitimacy, or at least of accepted permanence, which allows governments to impose burdens such as taxes and conscription on willing citizens. The material equipment for warfare is now widely available to private bodies, as are the means for financing non-state warfare. In this way, the balance between state and non-state organisations has changed.

Armed conflicts within states have become more serious and can continue for decades without any serious prospect of victory or settlement – Kashmir, Angola, Sri Lanka, Chechnya, Colombia. In extreme cases, as in parts of Africa, the state may have virtually ceased to exist; or it may, as in Colombia, no longer exercise power over part of its territory. Even in strong and stable states it has been difficult to eliminate small, unofficial armed groups, such as the IRA in Britain and ETA in Spain. The novelty of this situation is indicated by the fact that the most powerful state on the planet, faced with terrorist attack, feels obliged to launch a formal operation against a small, international, non-governmental organisation or network lacking both a territory and a recognisable army.

How do these changes affect the balance of war and peace in the coming century? I would rather not make predictions about wars that are likely to take place, or their possible outcomes.

However, both the structure of armed conflict and the methods of settlement have been changed profoundly by the transformation of the world system of sovereign states.

The dissolution of the USSR means that the Great Power system which governed international relations for almost two centuries and, with obvious exceptions, exercised some control over conflicts between states, no longer exists. Its disappearance has removed a major restraint on inter-state warfare and the armed intervention of states in the affairs of other states – foreign territorial borders were largely uncrossed by armed forces during the Cold War. The international system was potentially unstable even then, however, as a result of the multiplication of small, sometimes quite weak states which were nevertheless officially 'sovereign' members of the UN. The disintegration of the USSR and the European communist regimes plainly increased this instability. Separatist tendencies of varying strength in hitherto stable nation-states such as Britain, Spain, Belgium and Italy might well increase it further. At the same time, the number of private actors on the world scene has multiplied. Under these circumstances, it is not surprising that cross-border wars and armed interventions have increased since the end of the Cold War.

What mechanisms are there for controlling and settling such conflicts? The record is not promising. None of the armed conflicts of the 1990s ended with a stable settlement. The survival of Cold War institutions, assumptions and rhetoric has kept old suspicions alive, exacerbating the post-communist disintegration of south-east Europe and making the settlement of the region once known as Yugoslavia more difficult.

These Cold War assumptions, both ideological and power-political, will have to be dispensed with if we are to develop some means of controlling armed conflict. It is also evident that the US has failed, and will inevitably fail, to impose a new world order (of any kind) by unilateral force, however much power relations are skewed in its favour at present, and even if it is backed by an (inevitably short-lived) alliance. The international system will remain multilateral and its regulation will depend on the ability of several major units to agree with one another, even though none of these states enjoys military predominance. How far international military action taken by the US is dependent on the negotiated agreement of other states is already clear. It is also clear that the political settlement of wars, even those in which the US is involved, will be by negotiation and not by unilateral imposition. The era of wars ending in unconditional surrender will not return in the foreseeable future.

The role of existing international bodies, notably the UN, must also be rethought. Always present, and usually called upon, it has no defined role in the settlement of disputes. Its strategy and operation are always at the mercy of shifting power politics. The absence of an international intermediary genuinely considered neutral, and capable of taking action without prior authorisation by the Security Council, has been the most obvious gap in the system of dispute management.

Since the end of the Cold War the management of peace and war has been improvised. At best, as in the Balkans, armed conflicts have been stopped by outside armed intervention, and the status quo at the end of hostilities maintained by the armies of third parties. This sort of long-term intervention has been applied for many years by individual strong states in their sphere of influence (Syria in Lebanon, for instance). As a form of collective action, however, it has been used only by the US and its allies (sometimes under UN auspices, sometimes not). The result has so far been unsatisfactory for all parties. It commits the interveners to maintain troops indefinitely, and at disproportionate cost, in areas in which they have no particular interest and from which they derive no benefit. It makes them dependent on the passivity of the occupied population, which cannot be guaranteed; if there is armed resistance, small forces of armed 'peacekeepers' have to be replaced by much larger forces. Poor and weak countries may resent this kind of intervention as a reminder of the days of colonies and protectorates, especially when much of the local economy becomes parasitic on the needs of the occupying forces. Whether a general model for the future control of armed conflict can emerge from such interventions remains unclear.

The balance of war and peace in the twenty-first century will depend not on devising more effective mechanisms for negotiation and settlement but on internal stability and the avoidance of military conflict. With a few exceptions, the rivalries and frictions between existing states that led to armed conflict in the past are less likely to do so today. There are, for instance, comparatively few burning disputes between governments over international borders. On the other hand, internal conflicts can easily become violent. The main danger of war lies in the involvement of outside states or military actors in these conflicts.

States with thriving, stable economies and a relatively equitable distribution of goods among their inhabitants are likely to be less shaky socially and politically than poor, highly inegalitarian and economically unstable ones. A dramatic increase in economic and social inequality within, as well as between, countries will reduce the chances of peace. The avoidance or control of internal armed violence depends even more immediately, however, on the powers and effective performance of national governments and their legitimacy in the eyes of the majority of their inhabitants. No government today can take for granted the existence of an unarmed civilian population or the degree of public order long familiar in large parts of Europe. No government today is in a position to overlook or eliminate internal armed minorities. Yet the world is increasingly divided into states capable of administering their territories and citizens effectively – even when faced, as the UK was, by decades of armed action by an internal enemy – and into a growing number of territories bounded by officially recognised international frontiers, with national governments ranging from the weak and corrupt to the nonexistent. These zones produce bloody internal struggles and international conflicts, as we have seen in central Africa. There is, however, no immediate prospect for lasting improvement in such regions, and a further weakening of central government in unstable countries, or a further Balkanisation of the world map, would undoubtedly increase the dangers of armed conflict.

A tentative forecast: war in the twenty-first century is not likely to be as murderous as it was in the twentieth. But armed violence, creating disproportionate suffering and loss, will remain omnipresent and endemic – occasionally epidemic – in a large part of the world. The prospect of a century of peace is remote.

2

War, Peace and Hegemony at the Beginning of the Twenty-First Century

My subject is war, peace and hegemony, but I will approach present problems in the perspective of the past, as is the practice of historians. We cannot talk about the political future of the world unless we bear in mind that we are living through a period when history, that is to say the process of change in human life and society and the human impact on the global environment, has been accelerating at a dizzying pace. It is now proceeding at a speed which puts the future of both the human race and the natural environment at risk. When the Berlin Wall fell, an incautious American announced the end of history, so I hesitate to use a phrase so patently discredited. Nevertheless, in the middle of the last century we entered a new phase in world history which has brought to an end history as we have known it over the past ten thousand years – that is to say, since the invention of sedentary agriculture. We do not know where we are going.

I tried to sketch the outlines of this dramatic and sudden break in world history in my history of the 'short twentieth century'. The technological and productive transformations are obvious. Think only of the speed of the communications revolution, which has virtually abolished time and distance. The Internet was barely ten years old in 2004. I also singled out four social aspects of it that are relevant to the international future. These are the dramatic decline and fall of the peasantry, which had until the nineteenth century formed the great bulk of the human race as well as the foundation of its economy; the corresponding rise of a predominantly urban society, and especially the hyper-cities, with populations measured in eight digits; the replacement of a world of oral communication by a world of universal reading and writing by hand or machine; and finally, the transformation in the situation of women.

The fall in the numbers working in agriculture is obvious in the developed world. Today, the figure is 4 per cent of the occupied population in OECD (Organisation for Economic Co-operation and Development) countries, and 2 per cent in the US; and it is evident elsewhere. In the mid-1960s there were still five states in Europe with more than half the occupied population working in this area, eleven in the Americas, eighteen in Asia and, with three exceptions (Libya, Tunisia and South Africa), all of Africa. The situation today is dramatically different. For practical purposes, there is now no country in Europe or the Americas with more than half the occupied population working in agriculture, and the same is true in the Islamic world. Even Pakistan has fallen below the 50 per cent mark, while Turkey has moved from a peasant population of three quarters to one third. Even the major fortress of peasant agriculture in south-east Asia has been breached in several places: Indonesia is down from 67 per cent to 44 per cent, the Philippines from 53 per cent to 37 per cent, Thailand from 82 per cent to 46 per cent, and Malaysia from 51 per cent to 18 per cent. By 2006 even China, with 85 per cent of its population peasants in 1950, was down to 50 per cent or so. In fact, with the exception of most of sub-Saharan Africa, the only solid bastions of peasant society left – say, over 60 per cent of the occupied population in 2000 – are in the former south Asian empires of Britain and France – India, Bangladesh, Myanmar and the Indochinese countries. But, given the acceleration of industrialisation, for how long will this continue to be the case? In the late 1960s the farming population formed half of the population in Taiwan and South Korea; today that figure has fallen to 8 per cent and 10 per cent respectively. Within a few decades we will have ceased to be what humanity has been since its emergence, a species whose members are chiefly engaged in gathering, hunting or producing food.

We shall also cease to be an essentially rural species. In 1900 only 16 per cent of the world's population lived in towns; in 1950 that figure had risen to just under 26 per cent; today it is just under half (48 per cent).[1] In the developed countries and many other parts of the globe, the countryside, even in agriculturally productive areas, is a green desert in which human beings are hardly ever visible outside their cars and small settlements. But here extrapolation becomes more difficult. It is true that the old developed countries are heavily urbanised, but they are no longer typical of current urbanisation, which takes the form of a desperate flight from the countryside into what I have already called hyper-cities. What is happening to cities in the developed world, even the ones nominally growing, is the suburbanisation of areas around the original centre or centres. Today, only ten of the world's largest fifty cities and only two of the eighteen world cities whose population stands at ten million or more are in Europe and North America. The fastest-growing cities over one million are, with a single exception (Porto in Portugal), in Asia (twenty), Africa (six) and Latin America (five). Whatever its other consequences, this process dramatically changes the political balance between highly concentrated urban and geographically spread-out rural populations, especially in countries with elected representative assemblies or presidents.

I shall say little about the educational transformation, since the social and cultural effects of general literacy cannot easily be separated from the social and cultural effects of the sudden and utterly unprecedented revolution in the public and personal media of communication in which we are all engaged. Let me note only one significant fact. There are today twenty countries in which more than 55 per cent of the relevant age-groups continue studying after their secondary education, but with the single exception of South Korea, all of them are in Europe (old capitalist and ex-socialist), North America and Australasia. In its capacity to generate human capital, the old developed world still retains a substantial advantage over the major newcomers of the twenty-first century. How fast can Asia, and particularly India and China, catch up?

I want to say nothing here about the greatest single social

change of the past century, except for one observation to supplement what I have just said: the emancipation of women is best indicated by the degree to which they have caught up with or even surpassed the education of men. Need I say in India that there are parts of the world where it is still badly lagging behind?

Let me, from this bird's-eye perspective of the unprecedented transformations of the past half-century or so, descend for a closer look at the factors affecting war, peace and power at the outset of the twenty-first century. General trends are not necessarily guides to practical realities. It is evident, for instance, that in the course of the twentieth century the world's population (outside the Americas) ceased to be overwhelmingly ruled, as it were, from the top down, by hereditary princes or the agents of foreign powers. It now came to live in a collection of technically independent states whose governments claimed legitimacy by reference to 'the people' or 'the nation', in most cases (including even the so-called totalitarian regimes) claiming confirmation through real or bogus elections or plebiscites, and/or periodic mass public ceremonies that symbolised the bond between authority and 'the people'. One way or another, people have changed from being subjects to being citizens – including, in the twentieth century, not only men but women. But how close to reality does this get us today, when most governments have, technically speaking, variants of liberal-democratic constitutions with contested elections, though sometimes suspended by periods of military rule, that are deemed to be temporary but have often lasted a long time? Not very far.

Nevertheless, one general trend can be observed probably across most of the planet: the change in the position of the independent territorial state itself, which in the course of the twentieth century became the basic political and institutional unit in which human beings lived. In its original home, in the North Atlantic region, it was based on several innovations made since the French Revolution. It had the monopoly of the means of power and coercion – arms, armed men, prisons – and it exercised increasing control, through a central authority and its agents, over what took place on the territory of the state, based on a growing capacity to gather information. The scope of its activity and its impact on the daily life of its citizens grew, and so did its success in mobilising its inhabitants on the grounds of their loyalty to state and nation. This phase of state development reached its peak forty or so years ago.

Think, on the one hand, of the 'welfare state' of western Europe in the 1970s in which 'public consumption' – i.e. the share of the GDP used for public purposes, not private consumption or investment – amounted to between roughly 20 per cent and 30 per cent. Then think of the readiness of citizens not only to let public authorities tax them to raise such enormous sums, but actually to be conscripted to fight and die 'for their country' in their millions during the great wars of the last century. For more than two centuries, until the 1970s, this rise of the modern state had been continuous, proceeding irrespective of ideology and political organisation, be it liberal, social democratic, communist or fascist.

This is no longer the case. The trend is reversing. We have a rapidly globalising world economy based on transnational private firms that are doing their best to live outside the range of state law and taxes, which severely limits the ability of even big governments to control their national economies. Indeed, thanks to the prevailing theology of the free market, states are actually abandoning many of their most traditional direct activities – postal services, police, prisons, even vital parts of their armed forces – to profit-making private contractors. It has been estimated that thirty thousand or more such armed 'private contractors' are at present active in Iraq.[2] Thanks to this development and the flooding of the globe with small but highly effective weaponry during the Cold War, armed force is no longer monopolised by states and their agents. Even strong, stable states such as Britain, Spain and India have learned to live for long periods at a time with effectively indestructible, if not actually state-threatening, bodies of armed dissidents. We have seen, for various reasons, the rapid disintegration of numerous member-states of the UN, most but not all products of the disintegration of twentieth-century empires, in which the nominal governments are unable to administer or exercise actual control over much of state territory and population, or even their own institutions.

Almost equally striking is the decline in the acceptance of state legitimacy, of the voluntary acceptance of obligation to ruling authorities and their laws by those who live on their territories, whether as citizens or as subjects. Without the readiness of vast populations to accept as legitimate, for most of the time, any effectively established state power, even that of a comparative handful of foreigners, the era of nineteenth-/twentieth-century imperialism would have been impossible. Foreign powers were at a loss only in those rare zones where such readiness was unforthcoming, such as Afghanistan and Kurdistan. But, as Iraq demonstrates, the natural obedience of people in the face of power, even of overwhelming military superiority, has gone, and with it the return of empires. The obedience of citizens is eroding just as quickly. I very much doubt whether any state today could engage in major wars with conscript armies ready to fight and die 'for their country' to the bitter end. Few Western states can rely, as most so-called 'developed countries' once could, on a basically law-abiding and orderly population, except for the expected criminal or other fringes on the margins of the social order. The extraordinary rise of technological and other means of keeping citizens under surveillance at all times – CCTV cameras, phone-tapping, access to personal data and computers – has not made state and law more effective, though it has made citizens less free.

All this has been taking place in an era of dramatically accelerated globalisation, which is giving rise to regional disparities around the planet, for by its very nature globalisation produces unbalanced and asymmetric growth. It also underlines the contradiction between those aspects of contemporary life that are subject to globalisation and the pressures of global standardisation – science and technology, the economy, various technical infrastructures, and, to a lesser extent, cultural institutions – and those which are not, notably the state and politics. For instance, globalisation logically leads to an increased flow of labour migration from poorer to richer regions; but this produces political and social tension in many of the states affected, mostly the rich countries of the old North Atlantic region, even though in global terms this movement is modest: even today, only 3 per cent of the world's population lives outside the country of their birth. Unlike the movement of capital, commodities and communications, states and politics have so far put effective obstacles in the way of labour migrations.

The most striking new imbalance created by economic globalisation, apart from the dramatic de-industrialisation of the old Soviet and east European socialist economies in the 1990s, is the growing shift of the world economy's centre of gravity from the region bordering the North Atlantic to parts of Asia. This is still in its early stages, but accelerating. There can be no doubt that the growth of the world economy over the past ten years has been pulled along largely by the Asian dynamos, notably by the extraordinary rate of growth of industrial production in China, which saw a 30 per cent rise in 2003 compared with 3 per cent for the world and less than 0.5 per cent in North America and Germany.* Clearly this has not yet greatly changed the relative weight of Asia and the old North Atlantic – the US, the European Union and Japan between them continue to account for 70 per cent of the global GDP – but the sheer size of Asia is already making itself felt. In terms of purchasing power, south, south-east and east Asia already represent a market about two thirds larger than the US. How this global shift will affect the relative strength of the US economy is naturally a question central to the international prospects of the twenty-first century, and I shall return to it.

*Australia, France, Italy, the UK and Benelux had negative growth (CIA world Factbook up to 19 October 2004).

Let me now move even closer to the problem of war, peace and the possibility of international order in the new century. At first sight it would seem that the prospects of world peace must be superior to those of the twentieth century, with its unparalleled record of world wars and other theatres of death on an astronomic scale. And yet, a recent poll in Great Britain, which compared the answers of Britons in 2004 to questions first asked in 1954, reveals that the fear of world war today is actually greater than it was then.[3] That fear is largely due to the increasingly evident fact that we live in an era of endemic worldwide armed conflict, typically fought within states but magnified by foreign intervention. Though small in twentieth-century military terms, the impact of such conflicts on civilians – who have increasingly become their main victims – is relatively enormous, and long-lasting. Since the fall of the Berlin Wall, we once again live in an era of genocide and compulsory mass population transfers, as evidenced in parts of Africa, south-east Europe, and Asia. It has been estimated that at the end of 2003 there were perhaps thirty-eight million refugees inside and outside their own countries, which is a figure comparable to the vast numbers of displaced persons in the aftermath of the Second World War. One simple illustration: in 2000, the number of battle-related deaths in Burma was no more than five hundred, but the number of the 'internally displaced' – largely by the activities of the Myanmar army – was about one million.[4] Iraq confirms the point that small wars, by twentieth-century standards, produce vast catastrophes.

The typical twentieth-century form of warfare – that waged between states – has been declining sharply. At the moment, no such traditional inter-state war is taking place, although such conflicts cannot be excluded in various areas of Africa and Asia, or where the internal stability or cohesion of existing states is at risk. On the other hand, the danger of a major global war, probably arising out of the unwillingness of the US to accept the emergence of China as a rival superpower, has not receded, although it is not immediate. The chances of avoiding such a conflict are better than the chances of avoiding the Second World War were after 1929. Nevertheless, such a war remains a real possibility within the next few decades.

Even without traditional inter-state wars, small or large, few realistic observers today expect our century to bring a world without the constant presence of arms and violence. However, let us resist the rhetoric of irrational fear with which governments like President Bush's and Prime Minister Blair's seek to justify a policy of global empire. Except as a metaphor, there can be no such thing as a 'war against terror' or against terrorism, only against particular political actors who use what is a tactic, not a programme. As a tactic, terror is indiscriminate, and morally unacceptable, whether it is used by unofficial groups or states. The International Red Cross recognises the rising tide of barbarism for it condemns both sides in the Iraq War. There is also much fear that biological weapons may be used by small terrorist groups; but, alas, much less fear of the greater and unpredictable dangers posed if and when the new ability to manipulate the processes of life, including human life, escapes from control, as it surely will. However, the actual danger to world stability, or to any stable state, of the activities of the pan-Islamic terrorist networks against which the US proclaimed

its global war, or for that matter from the sum total of all the terrorist movements currently in action, is negligible. Though they
kill much larger numbers of people than their predecessors – if
many fewer than states – the risk to life they present is statisti-
cally minimal. For the purpose of military aggression, they
hardly count. Unless such groups were to gain access to nuclear
weapons – which is not unthinkable, but not an immediate
prospect either – terrorism will call for cool heads, not hysteria.

And yet, world disorder is real, and so is the prospect of another
century of armed conflict and human calamity. Can this be
brought under some kind of global control again, as it was for
all but thirty years during the 175 years from Waterloo to the
collapse of the USSR?

The problem is more difficult today for two reasons. First, the
much more rapidly growing inequalities created by uncontrolled
free-market globalisation are natural incubators of grievance
and instability. It has recently been observed that 'Not even the
most advanced military establishments could be expected to
cope with a general breakdown of legal order',[5] and the crisis of
states to which I referred earlier makes this likelier than it once
was. Second, there is no longer a plural international Great
Power system in a position to keep at bay a general collapse into
global war, except for the age of catastrophe from 1914 to 1945.
This system rested on the presumption, dating back to the
treaties that ended the Thirty Years War of the seventeenth
century, of a world of states whose relations were governed by
rules – notably non-interference in one another's internal
affairs – and on a sharp distinction between war and peace.

Neither is valid today. It also rested on the reality of a world of plural power, even in the small 'first division' of states, the handful of 'great powers', reduced after 1945 to two superpowers. None could prevail absolutely; outside much of the western hemisphere, even regional hegemony always proved to be temporary. The end of the USSR and the overwhelming military superiority of the US have ended this power system. What is more, US policy since 2002 has denounced both its treaty obligations and the conventions on which the international system was based on the strength of a probably lasting supremacy in high-tech offensive warfare, which has made it the only state capable of major military action in any part of the world at short notice.

US ideologists and their supporters see this as the opening of a new era of world peace and economic growth under a beneficent global American empire, which they compare, wrongly, to the Pax Britannica of the nineteenth-century British empire. Wrongly, because historically, empires have not created peace and stability in the world around them, as distinct from their own territories. If anything it was the absence of major international conflict that kept them in being, as was the case with the British empire. As for the good intentions of conquerors and their beneficent consequences, they belong in the sphere of imperial rhetoric. Empires have always justified themselves, sometimes quite sincerely, in moral terms, whether claiming to spread (their version of) civilisation or religion to the benighted, or (their version of) freedom to the victims of (someone else's) oppression, or today as champions of human rights. Patently, empires had some positive results. The claim that imperialism

43

brought modern ideas into a backward world, which has no validity today, was not entirely spurious in the nineteenth century. However, the claim that it significantly accelerated the economic growth of the imperial dependencies will not bear much examination, at least outside the areas of European overseas settlement. Between 1820 and 1950, the mean GDP per capita of twelve west European states multiplied by 4.5, whereas in India and Egypt it barely increased at all.[6] As for democracy, we all know that strong empires kept it at home; only declining ones conceded as little of it as they could.

But the real question is whether the historically unprecedented project of global domination by a single state is possible, and whether the admittedly overwhelming military superiority of the US is adequate to establish, and beyond this to maintain, it. The answer to both questions is no. Arms have often established empires, but it takes more than arms to maintain them, as that old saw dating back to Napoleon had it: 'You can do anything with bayonets except sit on them' – especially today, when even overwhelming military force no longer in itself produces tacit acquiescence. Actually, most historic empires have ruled indirectly, through native elites often operating native institutions. When they lose their capacity to win enough friends and collaborators among their subjects, arms are not enough. The French learned that even a million white settlers, an army of occupation of eight hundred thousand and the military defeat of the insurgency by systematic massacre and torture were not enough to keep Algeria French.

But why should we have to ask this question? This brings me to the puzzle with which I want to conclude my lecture. Why did the US abandon policies which maintained a real hegemony over the greater part of the globe, namely the non-communist and non-neutralist part, after 1945? Its capacity to exercise this hegemony did not rest on destroying its enemies or forcing its dependencies into line by the direct application of military force. The use of this was then limited by the fear of nuclear suicide. US military power was relevant to the hegemony only insofar as it was seen as preferable to other military powers – that is to say, during the Cold War, NATO Europe wanted its support against the armed might of the USSR.

The US hegemony of the second half of the last century rested not on bombs but on the enormous wealth of the US and the central role its giant economy played in the world, especially in the decades after 1945. Politically, it rested on a general consensus in the rich north that their societies were preferable to those under communist regimes; and, where there was no such consensus, as in Latin America, on alliances with national ruling elites and armies afraid of social revolution. Culturally, it rested on the attractions of the affluent consumer society enjoyed and propagated by the US, which had pioneered it, and Hollywood's world conquest. Ideologically, the US undoubtedly benefited as the champion and exemplar of 'freedom' against 'tyranny', except in those regions where it was only too obviously allied with the enemies of freedom.

All this could, indeed did, easily survive the end of the Cold War. Why should not others look for leadership to the superpower that represented what most other states now adopted, electoral democracy, to the greatest of the economic powers, committed to the neo-liberal ideology that was sweeping the globe? Its influence, and that of its ideologists and business executives, was immense. Its economy, though slowly losing its central role in the world and no longer dominant in industry, or even, since the 1980s, in direct foreign investments,* continued to be huge and to generate enormous wealth. Those who conducted its imperial policy had always been careful to cover the reality of US supremacy over its allies in what was a genuine 'coalition of the willing' with the emollient cream of tact. They knew that, even after the end of the USSR, the US was not alone in the world. But they also knew they were playing the global game with cards they had dealt and under rules that favoured them, and that no rival state of comparable strength and with global interests was likely to emerge. The first Gulf War, genuinely supported by the UN and the international community, and the immediate reaction to 9/11 demonstrated the post-Soviet strength of the US position.

It is the megalomaniac US policy since 9/11 that has very largely destroyed the political and ideological foundations of the former hegemonic influence and left the US with little to reinforce the heritage of the Cold War era but an admittedly frightening military power. There is no rationale for it. Probably for the first time in its history, an internationally almost isolated US is unpopular among most governments and peoples. Military strength underlines the economic vulnerability of a

*In 1980 it was of the order of 40 per cent of world direct foreign investments, between 1994 and 2005 it averaged only 14 per cent as against an average of 43 per cent for the European Union (UNCTAD *World Economic Outlook* [Geneva, 2006], 'Overview', p. 19).

US whose enormous trade deficit is maintained by Asian investors, whose economic interest in supporting a falling dollar is rapidly diminishing. It also underlines the relative economic clout of the European Union, Japan, east Asia, and even the organised bloc of Third World primary producers. In the World Trade Organisation, the US can no longer negotiate with clients. Indeed, may not the very rhetoric of aggression justified by implausible 'threats to America' indicate a basic sense of insecurity about the global future of the US?

Frankly, I can't make sense of what has happened in the US since 9/11 enabled a group of political crazies to realise long-held plans for an unaccompanied solo performance of world supremacy. I believe it indicates a growing crisis within US society, which finds expression in the most profound political and cultural division within that country since the Civil War, and a sharp geographical division between the globalised economy of the two seaboards and the vast, resentful hinterland, the culturally open big cities and the rest. Today, a radical right-wing regime seeks to mobilise 'true Americans' against some evil outside force, and against a world that does not recognise the uniqueness, the superiority, the manifest destiny of the US. What we must realise is that American global policy is aimed inwards, not outwards, however great and ruinous its impact on the rest of the world. It is not designed to produce either empire or effective hegemony. Nor was the Rumsfeld doctrine – quick wars against weak pushovers followed by quick withdrawals – designed for effective global conquest. Not that this makes it less dangerous – on the contrary: as is now evident, it spells instability, unpredictability, aggression and unintended, almost certainly disastrous, consequences. In effect, the most obvious danger of war today arises from the global ambitions of an uncontrollable and apparently irrational government in Washington.

How shall we live in this dangerous, unbalanced, explosive world in the midst of a major shifting of the social and political, national and international tectonic plates? If I were talking in London, I would warn Western liberal thinkers, however profoundly outraged by the deficiencies of human rights in various parts of the world, not to delude themselves into believing that American armed intervention abroad shares their motivation or is likely to bring about the results they would like. I hope this is not necessary in Delhi. As for governments, the best other states can do is to demonstrate the isolation, and therefore the limits, of US world power by refusing, firmly but politely, to join further initiatives proposed by Washington that might lead to military action, particularly in the Middle East and eastern Asia. To give the US the best chance of learning to return from megalomania to rational foreign policy is the most immediate and urgent task of international politics. For whether we like it or not, the US will remain a superpower, indeed an imperial power, even in what is evidently the era of its relative economic decline. Only, we hope, a less dangerous one.

3

Why American Hegemony Differs from Britain's Empire

History, we are told, is discourse. There is no understanding it unless we understand the language in which people think, talk and take decisions. Among the historians tempted by what is called 'the linguistic turn' there are even some who argue that it is the ideas and concepts expressed in the words characteristic of the period that explain what happened and why. The times we live in, and the subject of my Massey lecture, should be enough to make us sceptical of such propositions. Both are saturated with what the philosopher Thomas Hobbes called 'insignificant speech' (speech which means nothing) and its subvarieties 'euphemism' and George Orwell's 'newspeak' – namely, speech deliberately intended to mislead by misdescription. But unless the facts themselves change, no amount of changing names changes them.

The current debates about empire are good cases in point, even if we leave aside the element of advertising spin or plain

sanctimoniousness in the literature. They are about the implications of the present US government's claims to global
supremacy. Those who favour the idea tend to argue that
empires are good; those who do not tend to mobilise the long
tradition of anti-imperialist arguments. But these claims and
counter-claims are not really concerned with the actual history
of empires. They are trying to fit old names to historical
developments that don't necessarily fit old realities, which
makes little historical sense. Current debates are particularly
cloudy, because the nearest analogy to the world supremacy
to which the current US government is committed is a set of
words – 'empire', 'imperialism' – which are in flat contradiction
to the traditional political self-definition of the US, and which
acquired almost universal unpopularity in the twentieth
century. They are also in conflict with equally strongly held
positive beliefs in the US political value-system, such as 'self-
determination' and 'law', both domestic and international. Let
us not forget that both the League of Nations and the United
Nations were essentially projects launched and pressed through
by US presidents. It is also troublesome that there is no historical precedent for the global supremacy the US government
has been trying to establish, and it is quite clear to any good
historian and to all rational observers of the world scene that
this project will almost certainly fail. The most intelligent of the
neo-imperial school, that excellent historian Niall Ferguson,
has no doubts about this probable failure, though, unlike
people like me, he regrets it.[1]

Four developments lie behind the current attempts to revive
world empire as a model for the twenty-first century. The first is

the extraordinary acceleration of globalisation since the 1960s, and the tensions that have consequently arisen between the economic, technological, cultural and other aspects of this process and the one branch of human activity that has so far proved quite impermeable to it, namely politics. Globalisation in the currently dominant form of free-market capitalism has also brought about a spectacular and potentially explosive rise in social and economic inequality, within countries and internationally.

The second is the collapse of the international balance of power since the Second World War, which kept at bay both the danger of a global war and the collapse of large parts of the world into disorder or anarchy. The end of the USSR destroyed this balance, but I think it may have begun to fray from the late 1970s on. The basic rules of this system, established in the seventeenth century, were formally denounced by President Bush in 2002, namely that in principle sovereign states, acting officially, respected one another's borders and kept out of one another's internal affairs. Given the end of a stable superpower balance, how could the globe be politically stabilised? In more general terms, what would be the structure of an international system geared to a plurality of powers in which, at the end of the century, only one was left?

The third is the crisis in the ability of the so-called sovereign nation-state, which in the second half of the twentieth century became the almost universal form of government for the world's population, to carry out its basic functions of maintaining control over what happened on its territory. The world has entered the era of inadequate, and in many cases failing or failed, states.

This crisis also became acute from about 1970, when even strong, stable states such as the UK, Spain and France had to learn to live for decades with armed groups such as the IRA, ETA and Corsican separatists, groups they lacked the power to eliminate. The Uppsala databank recorded incidents of armed civil war between 2001 and 2004 in thirty-one of the world's sovereign states.[2]

The fourth is the return of mass human catastrophe, up to and including the wholesale expulsion of peoples and genocide, and with it the return of general fear. We have experienced the reappearance of something like the medieval Black Death in the AIDS pandemic; the global nervousness about the potential extension of an 'avian flu' that has to date killed no more than a few dozen humans; and the equivalent of eschatological hysteria in the tone of much public discussion on the effects of global warming. War and civil war have returned, even to Europe – there have been more wars since the fall of the Berlin Wall than during the whole of the Cold War period – and though the numbers who fight and their battle casualties are small compared to the mass wars of the twentieth century, their impact on the non-combatant population is disproportionately vast. At the end of 2004 it was estimated that there were nearly forty million refugees outside and increasingly inside their own countries,[3] which is comparable to the number of displaced persons in the aftermath of the Second World War. Concentrated as they are in a few zones of the globe, and now visible on screen in our living rooms almost as they occur, these images of desolation now have a far greater and more immediate public impact in the rich countries. Think only of the reaction to the Balkan wars in the

1990s. Surely, people in the rich countries of the globe felt, something must be done about the appalling situation into which many poorer areas seemed to be plunging?

In short, the world increasingly seemed to call for supranational solutions to supranational or transnational problems; but no global authorities were available with the ability to make policy decisions, let alone with the power to carry them out. Globalisation stops short when it comes to politics, domestic or international. The UN has no independent authority or power. It depends on the collective decision of states, and it can be blocked by the absolute veto of five of them. Even the international and financial organisations of the post-1945 world, such as the International Monetary Fund (IMF) and the World Bank, could take effective action only under Great Power patronage (the so-called 'Washington Consensus'). The one body that could not, GATT (since 1995 the World Trade Organisation, or WTO), has so far found state opposition an effective obstacle to agreement. The only effective actors are states. And in terms of conducting a major military action on a global scale, there is at present only one state capable of it, namely the US.

'The best case for empire is always the case for order' it has been said.[4] In an increasingly disorderly and unstable world it is natural to dream of some power capable of establishing order and stability. Empire is the name of that dream. It is a historical myth. The American empire, with its hopes of a Pax Americana, looks back to the assumed Pax Britannica, a period of globalisation and world peace in the nineteenth century associated with the assumed hegemony of the British empire, and this in turn looked back, and named itself after, the Pax Romana of the ancient Roman empire. But this is claptrap. If the term 'pax' has any meaning in this context, it refers to the claim to establish peace within an empire, not internationally. And even then it is largely phoney. The empires of history rarely ceased to conduct military operations on their territory, and certainly they did so on their frontiers at all times, only such operations rarely impinged on metropolitan civil life. In the era of nineteenth- and twentieth-century imperialism, they didn't tend to count wars against non-whites or other inferiors – Kipling's 'lesser breeds without the law' – as proper wars to which the usual rules applied. Hew Strachan rightly asks, 'Where were the prisoners taken in British colonial conflicts, other than the Boer War [which was seen as a war between whites]? What judicial processes were regularly applied?'[5] President Bush's 'unlawful combatants' in Afghanistan and Iraq, to whom neither law nor the Geneva Convention applies, have their imperialist precedents.

World or even regional peace has been beyond the power of all empires known to history so far, certainly beyond all the great powers of modern times. If Latin America has been the only part of the world largely immune to major international wars for almost two hundred years, it is not due to the Monroe doctrine, which was 'for decades . . . little more than a Yankee bluff',[6] or to US military power, which was never in a position directly to coerce any state in South America. Until the time of writing it was habitually used only in the dwarf states of Central America and the islands of the Caribbean, and then not always directly. Military intervention, including attempts to impose

54

'regime change', was practised in Mexico – or what was left of it after the war of 1848 – between 1913 and 1915 under President Wilson.[7] Disaster followed what has been described as his 'program of moral imperialism' which 'placed the weight of the United States behind a continuous, sometimes devious, effort to force the Mexican nation to meet his ill-conceived specifications'.[8] However, Washington has since then decided, wisely, not to play armed Pentagon games with the only large country in its Caribbean back yard. It was not US military power that brought about US domination of the western hemisphere.

Britain, of course, as the phrase 'splendid isolation' suggests, was always aware that it could not control the international power system of which it was a part, and had no significant military presence on the European continent. The British empire benefited enormously from the century of peace between the powers, but it did not create it. I would summarise the relations between empires, war and peace as follows. Empires were mainly built, like the British empire, by aggression and war. In turn, it was war – usually, as Niall Ferguson rightly points out, war between rival empires – that did for them. Winning big wars proved as fatal to empires as losing them – a lesson from the history of the British empire Washington might take to heart. International peace is not what they created, but what gave them a chance to survive. That superb book *Forgotten Armies* gives a vivid picture of how European power and hegemony in south-east Asia, apparently so splendid and secure, collapsed in a matter of weeks in 1941–2.[9]

All the same, leaving aside sixteenth-century Spain and perhaps seventeenth-century Holland, Britain from the mid-eighteenth to the mid-twentieth century and the US since then are the only examples of genuinely global empires, with global and not merely regional policy horizons and power resources – naval supremacy for nineteenth-century Britain, air supremacy for the twenty-first century US – backed by a unique world network of suitable bases. This was and is not enough, since empires depend not just on military victories or security but on lasting control. On the other hand, nineteenth-century Britain and the twentieth-century US also enjoyed an asset no previous empire had, or indeed could have had, in the absence of modern economic globalisation: they dominated the industrial world economy. They did so not only through the size of their productive apparatus as 'workshops of the world' – the US, at its peak in the 1920s and again after the Second World War, represented about 40 per cent of global industrial (manufacturing) output[10] and in 2005 was still the largest, though with only 22.4 per cent of 'manufacturing value added'[11] – both also did so as economic models, technical and organisational pioneers and trend-setters, and as the centres of the world system of financial and commodity flows, and the states whose financial and trade policies largely determined the shape of these flows.

Both, of course, have also exercised disproportionate cultural influence, not least through the globalisation of the English language. But cultural hegemony is not an indicator of imperial power, nor does it depend much on it. If it did, Italy, disunited, powerless and poor, would not have dominated international musical life and art from the fifteenth through the eighteenth centuries. Moreover, where cultural power survives the decline of the power and prestige of the states that once propagated it – the Roman empire, or the French absolute monarchy – it is merely a relic of the past, like the French-derived military nomenclature or the metric system.

We must, of course, distinguish the direct cultural effects of direct imperial rule from those of economic hegemony, and both again from independent post-imperial developments. The spread of baseball and cricket was indeed an imperial phenomenon, for these games are only played where once British soldiers or US Marines were stationed. But this does not explain the triumph of the truly global sports such as soccer, tennis and, for business executives, golf. They were all British nineteenth-century innovations, like practically all internationally practised sports, including alpinism and skiing. Some, such as thoroughbred racing, may owe their organisation and global spread to the international prestige of the nineteenth-century British ruling class, which also imposed its style of upper-class menswear on the world,[12] just as the prestige of Paris did with upper-class women's fashions. The origins of others, notably soccer, lie in the worldwide nineteenth-century diaspora of Britons hired to work for British firms abroad; yet others (golf), perhaps, to the disproportionate share of Scots in imperial and economic development. Yet they have long outgrown their historic origins. It would be absurd to see the next soccer World Cup as an example of the 'soft power' of Great Britain.

I now turn to the crucial differences between the two states. The potential size of the metropolis is the first obvious difference. Islands like Britain have fixed borders. Britain had no frontier in the American sense. Britain has been part of a European continental empire on occasions – in Roman times, after the Norman conquest, and, for a moment, when Mary Tudor married Philip of Spain – but never the base of such an empire. When the countries of Britain generated surplus populations, they migrated elsewhere or founded settlements overseas. The British Isles became a major source of emigrants. The US was and remains essentially a receiver, not a sender, of populations. It filled its empty spaces with its own growing population and with immigrants from abroad, until the 1880s mainly from north-western and west-central Europe. With Russia (apart from the Pale of Jewish settlement), it is the only major empire that never developed a significant emigrant diaspora. Unlike Russia since its fragmentation in 1991, the US still has not got one. Its expatriates form a lower percentage of the native-born inhabitants of any OECD country than those of any other OECD country except Japan.[13]

The US empire, it seems to me, is the logical by-product of this form of expansion across a continent. The young US saw its republic as co-terminous with all of North America. To settlers who brought to it European forms of farming population density, much of it seemed boundless and under-used. Indeed, given the rapid, unintended quasi-genocide of the indigenous population by the impact of European diseases, much of it soon became so. Even so, one is surprised today that Frederick Jackson Turner's famous 'frontier thesis' on the making of American history found no place at all for Native Americans, who, after all, had been very obviously present in the America of Fenimore Cooper.[14] North America was by no means 'virgin land',[15] but substituting the European form of economy for the indigenous and extensive use of the territory in both cases implied getting rid of the natives, even leaving aside the colonists' conviction that God had given the country exclusively to them. After all, the American Constitution specifically excluded the Native American from the body politic of 'the people which enjoyed the birthright of' the 'blessings of liberty'.[16] Of course effective elimination was possible only where the original population was relatively small, as in North America or Australia. Where it was not, as in Algeria, South Africa, Mexico and, as it turned out, Palestine, even large settler populations had to live with, or rather on top of, vast native populations.

Again unlike Britain and all other European states, the US never saw itself as one entity in an international system of rival political powers. That was precisely the system which the Monroe doctrine claimed to exclude from the western hemisphere. Within that hemisphere of decolonised dependencies, the US had no rival. Nor did it have a concept of a colonial dependency, since all parts of the North American continent were to be integrated as parts of the US sooner or later, even Canada, which it attempted but failed to detach from the British empire. So it had problems with taking over adjacent territories that did not fit the pattern, mostly because they were not colonised or colonisable by white anglos – Puerto Rico, Cuba and the Pacific dependencies, for example. Among such territories only Hawaii was to make it into a state. An independent slave South, being used to the difference between a free and a mass unfree population, and to integration into the British global trading system, might well have become more like a European empire, but it was the North that prevailed: free, protectionist, relying for its development on the unlimited mass home market. As it was, the characteristic form of US empire outside its continental heartland was not to be either like the British Commonwealth or the British colonial empire. It could not consider dominions – i.e. the gradual separation of areas of white settlement, with or without local natives (Canada, Australia, New Zealand, even South Africa) – because it sent no settlers abroad. In any case, since the North won the Civil War, the secession of any part of the Union was no longer legally and politically possible, or on the ideological agenda. The characteristic form of US power outside its own territory was not colonial, or indirect rule within a colonial framework of direct control, but a system of satellite or compliant states. This was all the more essential because US imperial power until the Second World War was not global, but only regional – effectively confined to the Caribbean and the Pacific. So it was never able to acquire a wholly owned network of military power bases comparable to the British one, most of which is still there, though it has now lost all its old significance. To this day several of the crucial bases of US power abroad are technically on the soil of some other state which might (like Uzbekistan) withdraw their use.

Second, the US is the child of a revolution – perhaps, as Hannah Arendt argued, of the most lasting revolution in the history of the revolutions of the modern era, the ones driven by the secular hopes of the eighteenth-century Enlightenment.[17] If it were to acquire an imperial mission, it would be based on the messianic implication of the basic conviction that its free society was superior to all others, and destined to become the global model. Its politics, as de Tocqueville saw, would inevitably be populist and anti-elitist. Both England and Scotland had their revolutions in the sixteenth and seventeenth centuries, but they did not last, and their effects were reabsorbed into a modernising but socially hierarchical capitalist regime, governed until well into the twentieth century by kinship networks of a landowning ruling class. Colonial empire could easily be fitted into this framework, as it was in Ireland. Britain certainly had a strong conviction of its superiority to other societies, but absolutely no messianic belief in, or particular desire for, the conversion of other peoples to the British ways of government, or even to the closest thing to an ideological national tradition, namely anti-Catholic Protestantism. The British empire was not built by or for missionaries; indeed, in its core dependency, India, the empire actively discouraged their activities.

Third, since the Domesday Book the kingdom of England, and after 1707 Britain, was built around a strong centre of law and government operating the oldest national state in Europe. Freedom, law and social hierarchy went with a uniquely sovereign state authority, 'the king in parliament'. Note that in 1707 England entered a Union with Scotland under a single central government, not as a federal arrangement, even though Scotland remained separate from England in every other respect – law, state religion, administrative structure, education, even the sound of its language. In the US, freedom is the adversary of central government, or indeed of any state authority, which is in any case deliberately crippled by the separation of powers. Compare the history of the US frontier with the very British history of its Canadian equivalent. The heroes of the US Wild West are gunmen who make their own law of the John Wayne kind in lawless territory; the heroes of the Canadian West are the Mounties, an armed federal police force founded in 1873 to maintain the state's law. After all, did not the British North America Act of 1867 that created the Dominion of Canada state its objective as 'peace, order and good government', not 'life, liberty and the pursuit of happiness'?

Let me briefly mention one further difference between the two countries considered as nations: age. Like a flag and an anthem, nation-states need a foundation myth for that modern construction, the nation, which is most conveniently provided by ancestral history. But the US could not use ancestral history as a foundation myth, as England and even revolutionary France could – as even Stalin could use Alexander Nevsky to mobilise Russian patriotism against the Germans. The US had no usable ancestors on its territory earlier than the first English settlers, since the Puritans defined themselves precisely as not being the Indians, and Native Americans, like slaves, were by definition outside the Founding Fathers' definition of 'the people'. Unlike the Spanish American Creoles, they could not mobilise the memories of indigenous empires – Aztecs, Incas – in their struggle for independence. They could not integrate the heroic traditions of Native American warrior peoples, though their intellectuals admired them, if only because settler policy drove the most obvious candidates for co-option into an all-American ideology, the Iroquois

Confederacy, mostly into alliance with the British. The only people linking its national identity to American Indians was European, the small and isolated Welsh, whose romantic explorers thought they had identified the descendants of Prince Madoc – who had once, they felt sure, discovered America before Columbus – as notionally Welsh-speaking Mandans on the Missouri.[18] And since the US was founded by revolution against Britain, the only continuity with the old country that was not shaken was cultural, or rather linguistic. But note that even here Noah Webster tried to break that continuity by insisting on a separate orthography.

So the national identity of the US could not be constructed out of a common English past, even before the mass immigration of non-Anglo-Saxons. It had to be primarily constructed out of its revolutionary ideology and its new republican institutions. Most European nations have so-called 'hereditary others' – permanent neighbours, sometimes with memories of centuries of conflict, against whom they define themselves. The US, whose existence has never been threatened by any war other than the Civil War, has only ideologically defined enemies: those who reject the American way of life, wherever they are.

As with states, so with empires. Here also Britain and the US are quite different. The empire – formal or informal – was an essential element both for Britain's economic development and its international power. It was not so for the US. What was crucial for the US was the initial decision to be not a state among other states, but a continental giant, eventually with a continental

population. The land and not the sea was central to its development. The US was expansionist from the start, but not in the
ways of overseas maritime empires like the sixteenth-century
Castilian and Portuguese, the seventeenth-century Dutch, and
the British, which could be and usually were based on states of
modest dimensions or populations. It was more like Russia,
expanding outwards across the plains from a central nucleus in
Muscovy until it could also claim to reach 'from sea to shining
sea', namely from the Baltic to the Black Sea and the Pacific.
The US without an empire would still be the state with by far
the largest population in the western hemisphere, and the third
most populated state on the globe. Even Russia, reduced as it
now is to what it was before Peter the Great, remains a relative
giant, not least in terms of the natural resources available
on its vast territory. Britain without its empire was and is just
one middle-sized economy among many, and knew itself to be
so even when it governed a quarter of the world's land and
population.

What is more to the point, because the British economy
was essentially linked to global economic transactions, the
British empire was in many respects a central element in the
development of the nineteenth-century world economy. This
was not because it was a formal empire. There are no significant British colonial territories in Latin America outside the
Caribbean area, and Britain deliberately refrained from using
its naval or military force to intervene there, though it could
easily have done so. Yet until the First World War Latin
America was far more a part of a British-oriented world economy than it was linked to the US: British investments were

more than twice as large as those of the US in 1914[19] and ran them close even in Mexico, where (with Cuba) American capital was concentrated.[20] In effect, nineteenth-century Britain was an economy complementary to the developing world. Through the 1950s, at least three quarters of Britain's enormous investments were in developing countries.[21] Even between the wars well over half of British exports went to the formal or informal British regions. That is why the British connection made the southern cone of Latin America prosperous while it lasted, while the US connection with Mexico has produced chiefly a source of cheap labour for the northern neighbour. With European and US industrialisation, Britain soon ceased to be the world's workshop, except in the construction of the international transportation structure, but it remained the world's trader, the world's banker, the world's capital exporter. Nor should we forget that at the peak of its economic supremacy Britain was in effect the world market for primary goods – food and raw materials. Modest as it was in size and population, as late as the 1880s it bought most of the internationally traded raw cotton and 35 per cent of internationally traded wool. It also consumed something like half of all internationally traded wheat and internationally traded meat, and most of its tea.[22]

The US economy had and has no such organic connection with the world economy. Being by far the largest industrial economy on the globe, it made, and still makes, its impact on it through sheer continental size and the Yankee originality in technology and business organisation that made it a model for the rest of the world from the 1870s on, and especially in the twentieth century, when it emerged as the first society of mass consumption. Until the period between the wars, heavily protected, it relied overwhelmingly on domestic resources and the domestic market. Unlike Britain, until the late twentieth century it was a relatively modest importer of commodities and a disproportionately small exporter of goods and capital: at the peak of its industrial power, in 1929, US economy exports amounted to 5 per cent of its GNP (1990 prices) as against 12.8 per cent for Germany, 13.3 per cent for the United Kingdom, 17.2 per cent for the Netherlands and 15.8 per cent for Canada.[23] Indeed, in spite of its global industrial primacy since the 1870s, with 29 per cent of world industrial output, its actual share of global exports did not equal that of Britain until the eve of the 1929 slump.[24] It remains one of the least trade-dependent economies in the world – much less so than even the euro area.[25] Although from the First World War on the US government encouraged American exporters with tax breaks and exemption from anti-trust law,[26] US enterprise did not seriously envisage penetrating into the European economies until the mid-1920s, and its advance was slowed by the Great Depression. Broadly speaking, the New World's economic conquest of the Old World is something that took place during the Cold War. There is no guarantee that it will last very long.

Unlike the worldwide advances of nineteenth-century Britain, this conquest was only partly the result of what might be called the global division of labour between industrialised and developing (primary-producing) countries. The great leap forward since the Second World War has been based on the increasingly globalised interchange between the similar and rival economies of developed industrial countries, which is why the gap between the developed and the poor worlds has widened so dramatically. But it is also why the plunge into free-market globalisation makes even the strongest national economy dependent on forces it cannot control.

This is not the place to analyse the recent shift in the geographical distribution of economic power from its old centres on both sides of the Atlantic to the regions of the Indo-Pacific oceans, nor their consequent vulnerability. Both are evident enough. The historic advantages that allowed most of the inhabitants of North America and the favoured parts of Europe, Japan and Australasia to enjoy as the new century began a GDP per capita at least five times as high as the global mean[27] and a standard of life princely by the standards of 1900, and under unprecedented conditions of social security, are eroding. Those who in the past benefited disproportionately from a globalised market economy may cease to do so, and those who pioneered globalisation may become its victims. The greatest of the American advertising agencies, J. Walter Thompson, which brought the twentieth-century way of marketing to the world, was taken over in 1987 by a British marketing service which now operates forty companies in eighty-three nations.

Faced with the industrialisation of Europe and the US, Victorian Britain – still massively industrialised, still the world's largest trader and investor – shifted its markets and capital investments to the formal and informal empire. The US of the early twenty-first century has no such option, and in any case could not, since it is no longer a major exporter of goods and capital, and pays for the goods it can no longer produce itself by going into debt to the new centres of world industry. It is the only major empire that has also been a major debtor. Indeed, with the exception of the seventy years between the First World War and 1988, the global bottom line of its economy has never been in credit.[28] The capital assets, visible and invisible, accumulated since 1945 by the US economy are large and not liable to rapid erosion. Nevertheless, US supremacy must be acutely vulnerable to its relative decline, and to the shift of industrial power, capital and high technology into Asia. In a globalised world, the 'soft power' of market and cultural Americanisation no longer reinforces US economic superiority. The US pioneered supermarkets, but in Latin America and China the running is made by the French Carrefour chain.

The American empire, unlike the British, has consistently had to rely on its political muscle. American global enterprise was mixed with politics from the start, or at least from the moment in 1916 when President Wilson addressed a convention of salesmen in Detroit and told them that America's 'democracy of business' had to take the lead in 'the struggle for the peaceful conquest of the world'.[29] No doubt its influence in the world rested both on being a model for business enterprise and its sheer size; yet it also rested on its fortunate immunity to the catastrophes of two world wars, which exhausted the economies of Europe and the Far East, while its own economy prospered. Nor were US governments unaware of the enormous boost this gave to dollar diplomacy. 'We have got to finance the world in some important degree,' thought Woodrow Wilson, 'and those who finance the world must understand it and rule it with their spirits and their minds.'[30]

During and after the Second World War, from the Lend-Lease of 1940 to the British Loan of 1946, Washington policy did not conceal that it aimed at the weakening of the British empire as well as victory over the Axis forces.

During the Cold War, the global growth of American enterprise took place under the patronage of the political project of the US, with which most American CEOs, like most Americans, identified themselves. In return, given its world power, the US government's conviction that American law ought to prevail in the dealings of Americans anywhere in the world put considerable political force behind it. In the (often misquoted) 1950s catchphrase, 'What's good for the country is good for General Motors, and vice versa.'[31] Of course the first mass consumer economy benefited enormously from the rise of affluent European mass consumer societies in the golden decades of the 1950s and 1960s. After all, it had developed the productive capacity, the big corporate producers, the institutions, the know-how and even the language of such society. As a French novelist said as early as 1930, advertising sold not only the goods but the adjectives to talk about them. This, rather than the lucky fact that thanks to the British empire English had the makings of a universal global language, is the essence of American cultural hegemony. Nevertheless, aside from its demonstration effect, the major contributions of the US to twentieth-century world economic development were politically anchored: the Marshall Plan in Europe, the occupation land reforms in Japan, the military orders in Asia for the Korean and, later, Vietnam wars. Without the Cold War political supremacy in the 'free world', would the sheer size of the US economy alone have been enough to establish as the global standard the US way of doing business, the US credit-rating agencies, accountancy firms and commercial contract practices, not to mention the 'Washington Consensus' for international financing? It may be doubted.

That is why the old British empire is not and cannot be a model for the American project of world supremacy – except in one respect. Britain knew its limits, and especially the limits, present and future, of its military power. Being a middleweight country which knew that it could not hold the world heavy-weight championship for ever, it was saved from the megalomania that is the occupational disease of would-be world conquerors. It occupied and ruled a larger part of the globe and its population than any state has ever done or is likely to do, but it knew it did not and could not rule the world, and it did not try. Its navy, which did indeed enjoy supremacy on the oceans for a long time, was not a force suited to this purpose. Once Britain had established its global position with successful aggression and war, it kept out of the politics of European states as much as it could, and altogether out of those in the western hemi-sphere. It tried to keep the rest of the world stable enough to proceed with its own business, but did not tell it what to do. When the age of Western overseas empires ended in the mid-twentieth century, Britain recognised 'the winds of change' earlier than other colonisers. And, because its economic position did not depend on imperial power but on trade, it adjusted more easily to its loss politically, as it had adjusted to the most dramatic setback in its earlier history, namely the loss of the American colonies.

Will the US learn this lesson, or will it be tempted to maintain an eroding global position by relying on politico-military force, and in so doing promote not global order but disorder, not global peace but conflict, not the advance of civilisation but of barbarism? That, as Hamlet said, is the question. Only the future will show. Since historians are, fortunately, not prophets, I am not professionally obliged to give you an answer.

4

On the End of Empires

Allow me to thank you for awarding me a doctorate h.c. at your distinguished university. Thessaloniki is a name that holds a great deal of meaning for me, not only as a Jew who cannot but recall the glories and tragedy of the greatest Jewish community in the Mediterranean, but as a socialist and a historian of labour. Greek socialism first joined the Second International through the Workers Federation of Salonica. Because Salonica was for so long a multinational city, its labour movement had – it had to have – a sense of internationalism. It tried to be a movement – I quote an early leader – 'to which all the nationalities can adhere without having to abandon their language and culture'. Salonica was the city that rose up against the government of Metaxas in 1936 and was the victim of his dictatorship. It is an honour to receive a degree from your university, but also to do so in a city such as this. Please accept my thanks.

New doctors are expected to give an inaugural lecture. I propose to make some remarks on the subject of the end of empires.

When I was born, all Europeans lived in states that were parts of empires in the traditional monarchical or the nineteenth-century colonial sense of the word, except the citizens of Switzerland, the three Scandinavian states and the former dependencies of the Ottoman empire in the Balkans – and some of these, for instance the inhabitants of Thessaloniki, had left the Ottoman empire only just before the First World War. The inhabitants of Africa lived under empires almost without exception, and so, without any exception, did the inhabitants of the Pacific and south-east Asian islands, large and small. But for the fact that the ancient Chinese empire had come to an end some six years before I was born, one might have said that all the countries of Asia were parts of empires, old and new, except perhaps Thailand (then known as Siam) and Afghanistan, maintaining a sort of independence between rival European powers. Only the Americas south of the US consisted primarily of states that neither had nor were colonial dependencies, even though they were certainly economically and culturally dependent.

In the course of my lifetime, all this has gone. The first war broke the Habsburg empire into fragments, and completed the break-up of the Ottoman empire. But for the October Revolution, this would also have been the fate of the empire of the Russian tsar, though it was severely weakened, as was the German empire, which lost both the imperial title and its colonies. The Second World War destroyed the imperial potential of Germany, which had been briefly realised under Adolf

Hitler. It destroyed, too, the colonial empires of the imperialist era, great and small: the British, French and Japanese, the Dutch and Portuguese, the Belgian, and what little remained of the Spanish. (Incidentally, it also brought about the end of the US's relatively brief excursion into formal colonialism on the European model, in the Philippines and a few other territories.) Finally, at the end of the last century, the collapse of European communist regimes brought to an end both Russia as a single multinational entity as it had existed under the tsars and the more short-lived Soviet empire in east-central Europe. The metropoles have lost their power, as they have lost their dependencies. Only one potential imperial power remains.

Thirty years ago, most of us welcomed this dramatic change in the political face of the globe; many of us still do. However, today we look back on it from a troubled new century that seems to lack the relative order and predictability of the Cold War era. The era of empires has gone, but so far nothing has effectively replaced it. The number of independent states has quadrupled since 1913, most of them the debris of former empires; but while in theory we now live in the world of free nation-states which according to Presidents Wilson and F.D. Roosevelt was to replace the world of empires, in practice we live in what we can now recognise as a deeply unstable form of global disorder internationally and within states. A number, probably a growing number, of these political entities appear incapable of carrying on the essential functions of territorial states, or are threatened with disintegration by secessionist movements. What is more, since the end of the Cold War we have lived in an era when uncontrollable or barely controllable armed conflict has become endemic in large areas of Asia, Africa, Europe and parts of the Pacific. Massacre amounting to genocide and the mass expulsion of populations ('ethnic cleansing') are once again taking place on a scale not seen since the years immediately following the Second World War. Should we wonder that in some countries the survivors of former empires regret their passing?

How should these empires be remembered? The nature of official and popular memory depends to some extent on the length of time that has elapsed since an empire's disappearance, and whether it has left any inheritors. The Roman empire, both in its western and eastern form, was so completely destroyed, and destroyed so long ago, that it has no inheritor, though the mark it left on the world, even outside the area it once occupied, is enormous. Alexander's is gone for ever; so is Genghis Khan's and Timur's; so are the empires of the Ummayads and Abbasids. More recently, the Habsburg empire was so completely destroyed in 1918, and is so completely a-national in structure, that it has no effective continuity with the small nation-state now called Austria. However, often there is some continuity, especially as the end of so many empires is so recent, and has usually been accompanied or followed in the former metropolitan states by periods of considerable political and psychological stress. True, today no state that once ruled over a colonial empire intends or has any hope of restoration; but where the metropoles of former empires survive as effective states, usually as nation-states, there is a tendency among them after a while to look back on times of past greatness with pride and nostalgia. There is also an understandable temptation to exaggerate the benefits the empire is said to have conferred on its subjects while it existed, such as law and order within its territories, and, with more justification, the fact that several (but not all) vanished empires were more tolerant of ethnic, linguistic and religious multiplicity than the nation-states that succeeded them. Nevertheless, as a writer on empires points out when reviewing Professor Mazower's remarkable social history of your own city, 'this theory of empire is too good to be true'.[1] The reality of empires should not be in the hands of selective nostalgia.

Only one collective form of imperial memory has practical implications today. This is the feeling that the superior power of empires to conquer and rule the world was based on superior civilisation, easily identified with moral or even racial superiority. In the nineteenth century both tended to go together, but the historical experience of Nazi Germany has eliminated from polite discourse racial/ethnic claims to superiority. However, the tacit rather than openly articulated Western claim of moral superiority remains. It finds expression in the conviction that our values and institutions are superior to others', and may, or even should, be imposed on them to their benefit, if necessary by force of arms.

The claim that historically empires and imperialism brought civilisation to backward peoples and substituted order for anarchy is doubtful, though not entirely spurious. From the third to the seventeenth centuries of our era, most empires were the products of military conquest by warrior tribes from the outer edges of the Asian and Mediterranean civilisations. Culturally backward, they brought little to the conquered and often more advanced lands but their swords and, if they wanted to last, a willingness to use the infrastructure and the expertise of those they had defeated. Only the Arabs, who carried their written language and their new religion with them, brought something new. The Europeans who colonised the Americas, Africa and the Pacific were indeed technologically superior to the local societies, though until the nineteenth century not to Asian and some Islamic ones. Colonial territories were indeed eventually integrated into an occidentalo-centric world economy. But we may well ask how positive is the balance-sheet of the colonial era for the inhabitants of the Americas, other than the descendants of the European immigrants who settled there. Or, to take a more recent case, for the inhabitants of sub-Saharan Africa.

The memory of empire among its former subjects is more ambiguous. Most colonies or other dependencies of former empires have been transformed into independent states, which like all states, however new and unprecedented, need a history as well as a flag. So their memory of the former empire is almost always dominated by the history of the creation of the new state, which tends to take the form of a foundation myth of struggle and liberation. Not unnaturally, it also tends to take a uniformly negative view of the era of imperial rule. In most cases this calls for historical scepticism. Such narratives tend to exaggerate the independent role of the forces of liberation, to underestimate the local forces not involved in the liberation movements, and to oversimplify the relationship between an empire and its subject population. Even in countries with a long history of liberation struggle, separation from empire usually was a more complex process than official nationalist history allows. The truth is that what brought empires to an end was rarely the revolt of their subject peoples alone.

The relationship between empires and their subjects is complex, because the foundation of the power of lasting empires is also complex. Brief periods of foreign occupation may rest essentially on military power and the willingness to use coercion and terror, but these alone cannot guarantee durable foreign rule, especially when that rule is exercised, as it almost always has been, by relatively, and indeed usually absolutely, tiny numbers of foreigners. Let us remember that the number of British civilians engaged in governing the four hundred million people of the Indian empire was never more than about ten thousand. Historically, empires may have been conquered by military force and established by terror – 'shock and awe' in the phrase of the US Pentagon – but if they wanted to last, they had to rely on two main instruments: co-operation with local interests and the legitimacy of effective power while also exploiting the disunity of their adversaries and their subjects (*divide et impera*). The present situation in Iraq illustrates the difficulties even the most powerful occupier will face when these are absent.

But for that very reason the old era of empires cannot be revived, least of all by a single superpower. One of the major assets of Western imperialism, formal or informal, was that in the first instance 'Westernisation' was the only form in which backward economies could be modernised and weak states strengthened. This provided Western empires or modernising metropoles of traditional empires with the built-in goodwill of such local elites as were interested in overcoming local back-wardness. This was so even when the indigenous modernisers eventually turned against foreign rule, as in India and Egypt. Paradoxically, the Indian national anthem was written by a senior native member of the Indian Civil Service of the British Raj. Yet the globalisation of the industrial economy has made modernisation international. South Korea has little to learn from the US, which imports its software experts from India and exports its office-work to Sri Lanka, while Brazil produces not only coffee but executive jets. Asians may still find it useful to send their children to study in the West, often to be taught there by emigrant Asian academics, but the presence of Westerners in their countries, let alone local political power and influence, is no longer needed to modernise their societies.

Yet would-be empires face an even greater handicap. They can no longer rely on the obedience of their subjects. And, thanks to the heritage of the Cold War, those who refuse to obey now have access to weapons sufficiently powerful to hold strong states at bay. In the past, countries could be ruled by a comparative handful of foreigners because the rule of any regime with effective power was accepted by people used to being ruled from above, whether by natives or foreigners. Imperial rule, once established, was likely to be resisted only by peoples who rejected any central state power, indigenous or foreign, and who usually lived in zones like the Afghan, Berber or Kurdish mountains, beyond effective civilian control. And even these knew that they had to co-exist with the greater power of sultan, tsar and raja. Today, as the former French territories in Africa demonstrate, the presence of a few French troops alone is no longer enough to maintain local regimes, as it was for decades after formal decolonisation. Today, the full armed power of governments has proved incapable of maintaining unchallenged control of their territory for decades – in Sri Lanka, in India's Kashmir, in Colombia, in the Gaza Strip and the West Bank, or, for that matter, in parts of Belfast. There is, indeed, a general crisis of state power and state legitimacy, even on the home territories of old and stable European states such as Spain and the United Kingdom.

In these circumstances, there is no prospect of a return to the imperial world of the past, let alone the prospect of a lasting global imperial hegemony, unprecedented in history, by a single state, the US, however great its military force. The age of empires is dead. We shall have to find another way of organising the globalised world of the twenty-first century.

5

Nations and Nationalism in the New Century

There is now an extensive scholarly literature on the nature and history of nations and nationalism, mainly produced since the publication of a number of influential texts in the 1980s.[1] Debate on these matters has been continuous since then, and as we enter the twenty-first century, it may be worth pausing to consider the striking historic changes of the last few decades that have affected this debate. Chief among these is the onset of an era of international instability since 1989 whose end cannot yet be foreseen. This is the purpose of the present note.

It is now easier to assess the far-reaching consequences of the end of the Cold War and the USSR and its sphere of influence, both of which can be seen in retrospect as politically stabilising forces. Since 1989 an international power system has ceased to exist, for the first time in European history since the eighteenth century. Unilateral attempts to establish a global order have so far not succeeded. Meanwhile, the 1990s saw a notable Balkanisation of large parts of the old world, mainly through the disintegration of the USSR and the communist regimes in the Balkans – that is to say, the largest increase in the number of internationally recognised sovereign states since the decolonisation of the European empires of the imperialist era between the end of the Second World War and the 1970s. The membership of the United Nations has risen by thirty-three states (or over 20 per cent) since 1988. The period has also seen the rise of the so-called 'failed states', i.e. a virtual collapse of effective central government, or a situation of endemic internal armed conflict, in some regions in several nominally independent states, notably in Africa and the ex-communist successor states, but also in at least one region of Latin America. Indeed, for a few years after the end of the USSR even its major successor state, the Russian Federation, looked as though it might come close to joining the ranks of 'failed states', but the efforts of President Putin's government to restore effective government power over the entire state territory appear to have been successful, except in Chechnya. Nevertheless, large regions of the globe remain both internationally and internally unstable.

That instability is dramatically increased by the decline of the monopoly of armed force, which was so long in the hands of states. The Cold War left behind an enormous worldwide supply of small but very powerful weapons and other devices of destruction for non-governmental use, easily acquired with the financial resources available from the huge and uncontrollable para-legal sector of the dramatically expanded global capitalist economy. The so-called 'asymmetrical warfare' of current American strategic debates consists precisely of such non-state armed groups capable of maintaining themselves against foreign or domestic state power almost indefinitely.

One disturbing result of these developments is a global relapse into the first major epidemic of massacre, genocide and 'ethnic cleansing' since the immediate years after the Second World War. The eight hundred thousand slaughtered in Rwanda in 1994 are only the greatest of a series of mass murders and the even more persistent mass expulsions of the 1990s – in west and central Africa, in the Sudan, in the ruins of what had once been Communist Yugoslavia, in Transcaucasia, in the Middle East. The number of the dead and maimed, swollen as it was by the almost unbroken series of wars and civil wars of the 1990s, may still be impossible to estimate, but the consequent flood of refugees and other displaced persons in this miserable decade is certainly of the same order of magnitude, relative to the populations concerned, as in the years of the Second World War and its aftermath. In 2005, the UN High Commissioner for Refugees estimated that the organisation was concerned with a world total of 20.8 million, overwhelmingly in (or from) certain regions in western and south central Asia, Africa and south-eastern Europe; but the Church World Service's *Statistics of Uprooted Peoples* (December 2005) registered thirty-three million, and another estimate added a further two million to that.

During the Cold War, the duopoly of the superpowers had, on the whole, maintained the integrity of the world's state frontiers against internal and external threats. Since 1989 no such a priori defences have stood in the way of the disintegration of central state power in many of the nominally independent and sovereign states established between 1945 and 2000, and even some long-established ones, such as Colombia. Large parts of the world have therefore found themselves reverting to a situation in which effective strong and stable states, for various reasons or under various pretexts, intervene by force of arms in regions no longer effectively protected by international stability or controlled by their own governments. In important regions such as the Islamic world, resentment of invading and occupying Westerners after a comparatively brief period of emancipation from imperial control has, once again, become a politically powerful factor.

The second new element affecting the problem of nations and nationalism is the extraordinary acceleration of the process of globalisation in recent decades and its effect on the movement and mobility of human beings. It affects both temporary and lasting movements across state frontiers, and the scale of both is without precedent. At the end of the century *c.* 2600 million human beings per annum were transported by the world's airlines, or almost one air journey for every two inhabitants of the globe. As for the globalisation of international mass migration – mainly, as usual, from poor to rich economies – its scale is particularly clear in the case of countries such as the US, Canada and Australia, which have imposed no major limits on immigration. These three countries received almost twenty-two million immigrants from all parts of the globe between 1974 and 1998, a larger total than in the great era of pre-1914 immigration and almost twice the pre-1914 rate of influx per year.[2] In the years 1998 to 2001 alone, these three countries had an inflow of 3.6 million. But even western Europe, long a region of mass emigration, received almost eleven million strangers during that period. The influx accelerated into the new century. From 1999 to 2001, a total of *c*. 4.5 million entered the fifteen states of the European Union. To take but one example, the number of foreigners legally living in Spain more than trebled between 1996 and 2003 from half a million to 1.6 million, two thirds of them from outside the European Union, mostly Africa and South America.[3] The astonishing cosmopolitisation of great cities in the wealthy countries is a visible consequence. In short, in Europe, the original home of nationalism, the transformations of the world economy are making short work of what the wars of the twentieth century, with their genocides and mass population transfers, appeared to produce, namely a mosaic of ethnically homogeneous nation-states.

Thanks to the technological revolution in the cost and speed of transport and communications, the twenty-first century's long-term emigrants, unlike those of the nineteenth century, are no longer effectively cut off from their original homeland, except by letters, occasional visits or the 'long-distance nationalism' of emigrant organisations financing political bodies in their native country. Prosperous emigrants now commute between homes, or even jobs and businesses, in the old country and the new. North American airports on public holidays are inundated with Central Americans taking a trip to some Salvadorean or Guatemaltec village, bringing electronic gifts. Family occasions in one country, old or new, are attended at short notice by friends and relatives from three continents. Even the poorest can telephone cheaply to Bangladesh or Senegal and send those regular remittances which doubled between

2001 and 2006 and now maintain the national economies of their homelands, providing something in the order of 10 per cent of the GDP in North Africa and the Philippines, 10 to 16 per cent in Central America and the Caribbean, and even higher figures in a number of unhappy economies in countries such as Jordan, Lebanon and Haiti.[4] The number of countries permitting dual nationality doubled in the ten years up to 2004, when it was available in ninety-three states.[5] In effect, emigration no longer implies a lasting choice between countries.

It is not yet possible to judge the effect of this extraordinary mobility across borders on older concepts of nations and nationalism, but there is no doubt that they will be substantial. As Benedict Anderson has acutely observed, the crucial document of twenty-first-century identity is not the nation-state's birth certificate, but the document of international identity – the passport. How far has actual or potential plural nationality – for example, the American background of politicians in former communist states, the identification of US Jews with Israeli governments – affected, or how far is it likely to affect, citizen loyalty to a nation-state?[6] What is the meaning of 'citizenship' rights and obligations in states where a substantial percentage of the inhabitants are absent from the national territory at any one time, and a substantial proportion of permanent residents have inferior rights to indigenous citizens? Given the scale of legal and clandestine movement, what is the effect of the state's declining power to control what happens on its territory, or even, as the growing unreliability of censuses in the US and Britain suggests, to know who is present on its territory? These are questions we must ask, but cannot as yet answer.

The third element, xenophobia, is not new, but its scale and implications were underestimated in my own work on modern nationalism. In the historic European homelands of nations and nationalism, and to a lesser extent in countries such as the US largely formed by mass immigration, the new globalisation of movement has reinforced the long tradition of popular economic hostility to mass immigration and resistance to perceived threats to group cultural identity. The sheer force of xenophobia is indicated by the fact that the ideology of globalised free-market capitalism, which has captured the dominant national governments and international institutions, has utterly failed to establish the free international movement of labour, unlike those of capital and trade. No democratic government could afford to support it. However, this evident rise of xenophobia reflects the social cataclysms and moral disintegration of the late twentieth and twenty-first centuries as well as mass international population movements. The combination is naturally explosive, particularly in ethnically, confessionally and culturally homogeneous countries and regions unused to major influxes of strangers. This is why a proposal to transform Protestant chapels that are no longer used into mosques for a flourishing religion of immigrants has recently caused a brief uproar in as tranquil and tolerant a country as Norway, and why this reaction will almost certainly be understood by every reader of this book in the old European homelands of nationalism.

The dialectics of the relations between globalisation, national identity and xenophobia are dramatically illustrated in the public activity that combines all three: football. For, thanks to

global television, this universally popular sport has been transformed into a worldwide capitalist industrial complex (though,
by comparison with other global business activities, of relatively
modest size). As has been well said, 'De cette dichotomie, entre
d'une part le "national", dernier refuge des passions du monde
ancien, et d'autre part le "transnational", tremplin de l'ultra-
libéralisme du monde nouveau, il résulte, pour l'amateur de
football tout autant que pour les milieux qui gravitent autour de
ce sport, une véritable schizophrénie, extrêmement com-
plexe . . . qui illustre finalement à la perfection le monde
ambivalent dans lequel nous vivons tous.'[7] ['Torn between
national feeling, the last refuge of the emotions of the old world,
and transnationality, springboard of the new world, football
fans and all those who gravitate round this sport suffer from a
veritable schizophrenia. Its extreme complexity provides a per-
fect illustration of the ambivalence of the world in which we all
live.']

Almost since this sport acquired a mass public, it has been
the catalyst of two forms of group identification: local (with the
club) and national (with the national team drawn from club
players). In the past these were complementary, but the transformation of football into a global business, and above all the
extraordinarily rapid rise of a global market for players in the
1980s and 1990s (especially after the 1995 Bosman Ruling of
the European Court of Justice),[8] has made the interests of
nation and globalised business, politics, economics and popular
sentiment increasingly incompatible. Essentially, the global football business is dominated by the imperialism of a few capitalist
enterprises with global brand names – a small number of

super-clubs based in a few European countries* competing against one another both in national and (preferably) international leagues. Their teams are recruited transnationally. Often only a minority, sometimes a small minority, of their players are natives of the country in which the club is situated. Since the 1980s they have been increasingly drawn from non-Europeans, especially Africans, of whom three thousand were said to be playing in European leagues in 2002.

The effect of this development has been threefold. So far as the clubs are concerned, it has severely weakened the position of all those not in the ensemble of international super-leagues and super-contests, but especially those in countries with heavy exports of players, notably the Americas and Africa – as evidenced by the crisis in the formerly proud football clubs of Brazil and Argentina.[9] Within Europe, the smaller clubs maintain themselves against the competition of the giants largely by buying players cheap – talented overseas beginners, for example – in the hope of reselling the discovered stars to the super-clubs. Youngsters from Namibia play in Bulgaria, from Niger in Luxembourg and Poland, from Sudan in Hungary, from Zimbabwe in Poland.

The second effect is that the transnational logic of business enterprise has come into conflict with football as an expression of national identity, both because it tends to favour international contests between super-clubs over the traditional

---

*The eighteen clubs seeking to establish a European 'Super League' comprised three each from England, Italy, Spain, Germany and France, two from the Netherlands, and one from Portugal. It should be noted that there was a similar move from clubs in the smaller European leagues to favour an 'Atlantic League'.

national leagues and cups, and because the interests of the super-clubs compete with those of the national teams that carry the full political and emotional load of national identity, but which must be recruited from players with the requisite state passport. Unlike the super-clubs, which may actually sometimes be stronger than their national teams, they are impermanent. They are today likely to be collections of players, many – in extreme cases like Brazil, most – of whom play at some overseas club which loses money for every day they are absent during the minimum periods needed to train and play together as a national team. From the point of view of super-clubs and super-players, club tends to be more important than country. Yet the non-economic imperatives of national identity have been strong enough to assert themselves within the game, indeed strong enough to establish the contest of national football teams, the World Cup, as the most powerful single element in the global economic presence of football. Indeed, for several of the African and some of the Asian countries whose players have now become famous (and rich) in the major club economy, the existence of a national football team has, sometimes for the first time, established a national identity separate from local, tribal or confessional identities. For 'the imagined community of millions seems more real as a team of eleven named people'.[10] Indeed, even the recently reviving nationalism of the English found its first public expression in the mass public exhibition of the flag of the international English (as distinct from the Scottish, Welsh and Northern Irish) football team.

The third effect may be seen in the increasing prominence of xenophobic and racist behaviour among the (overwhelmingly male) *tifosi*, notably of the imperial countries. They are torn between pride in their super-clubs or national teams (including their foreign or black players) and the growing prominence on their national scene of competitors from peoples so long thought of as inferior. The periodic racist outbursts in the football stadia of countries not previously thought of as racist – Spain, the Netherlands – and the association of football hooliganism with the politics of the extreme right are expressions of these tensions.

However, as already noted, xenophobia also reflects the crisis of a culturally defined national identity in nation-states under conditions of universal education and access to the media, and at a time when the politics of exclusive collective identity, whether ethnic, religious or of gender and lifestyle, seek a factitious regeneration of *Gemeinschaft* in an increasingly remote *Gesellschaft*. The process which turned peasants into Frenchmen and immigrants into American citizens is reversing, and it crumbles larger nation-state identities into self-regarding group identities, or even into the a-national private identities of *ubi bene ibi patria*. And this in turn reflects, not least, the diminishing legitimacy of the nation-state for those who inhabit its territory, and the diminishing demands it can make on its citizens. If twenty-first-century states now prefer to fight their wars with professional armies, or even with private contractors of war services, it is not only for technical reasons, but because citizens can no longer be relied upon to be conscripted in their millions to die in battle for their fatherlands. Men and women may be prepared to die (or more likely to kill) for money or for something smaller, or for something larger, but in the original homelands of the nation, no longer for the nation-state.

What, if anything, will replace it as a general model of popular government in the twenty-first century? We do not know.

6

The Prospects of Democracy

There are words nobody likes to be associated with in public, such as racism and imperialism. On the other hand, there are others for which everyone is anxious to demonstrate enthusiasm, such as mothers and the environment. Democracy is one of these. You may recall that in the days of what used to be called 'really existing socialism' even the most implausible regimes laid claim to it in their official titles, such as North Korea, Pol Pot's Cambodia, and Yemen. Today, of course, it is impossible, outside some Islamic theocracies and Asian hereditary kingdoms and sheikhdoms, to find any regime that does not pay official tribute, in constitution and editorial, to competitively elected assemblies or presidents. Any state which possesses these attributes is officially considered superior to any state which does not, for example post-Soviet Georgia to Soviet Georgia, a corrupt civilian Pakistan to the military regime there. Irrespective of history and culture, the constitutional features common to Sweden, Papua New Guinea and Sierra Leone (when elected presidents can be found there) officially put them into one class, Pakistan and Cuba in the other. This is why rational public discussion of democracy is both necessary and unusually difficult.

Moreover, all rhetoric aside, as Professor John Dunn points out, today, however briefly, 'for the first time in human history there is a single clearly dominant state form, the modern constitutional representative democratic republic',[1] even though it must also be pointed out that the highest proportion of stable political systems which would be regarded as democratic by impartial observers can today be found in monarchies, for these appear to have survived best in this political environment, namely in the European Union and Japan.

Indeed, in the political discourse of our times, almost all of which can be described in the words of the great Thomas Hobbes's Leviathan as 'insignificant speech', the word 'democracy' means this standard state model; that is to say, a constitutional state offering to guarantee the rule of law and various civil and political rights and freedoms, and governed by authorities, which must include representative assemblies, elected by universal suffrage and numerical majorities of all citizens, in elections held at regular intervals between competing candidates and/or organisations. Historians and political scientists may correctly remind us that this is not the original meaning of democracy, and is certainly not the only one. For my present purposes that is beside the point. 'Liberal democracy' is what we are confronted with today, and its prospects are the subject of my discussion.

It may be slightly more to the point to recall that there is no necessary or logical connection between the various components of the conglomerate that makes up 'liberal democracy'. Non-democratic states may be built on the principle of the *Rechtstaat*, or rule of law, as Prussia and imperial Germany undoubtedly were. Constitutions, even effective and operational constitutions, do not have to be democratic. We have known since de Tocqueville and John Stuart Mill that freedom and toleration for minorities are often more threatened than protected by democracy. We have also known since Napoleon III that regimes that come to power by *coup d'état* can continue to win genuine majorities by successive appeals to universal (male) suffrage. And – to choose only some recent examples – neither South Korea nor Chile in the 1970s and 1980s suggests an organic connection between capitalism and democracy, though the two are treated almost as Siamese twins in the political rhetoric of the US. Still, since we are dealing in political and social practice today and not theory, these may be regarded as academic quibbles, except insofar as they suggest that much of the case for liberal democracy rests on its constitutional liberal component rather than its democratic, or more precisely electoral, component. The case for free voting is not that it guarantees rights but that it enables the people (in theory) to get rid of unpopular governments.

Three critical observations are more immediately relevant, however.

The first is obvious, but its significance is not always recognised. Liberal democracy, like any other form of political regime, requires a political unit within which it can be exercised, normally the kind of state usually known as a 'nation-state'. It is not applicable to fields where no such unit exists, or looks like coming into existence, notably to global affairs, however urgently these may concern us. Whatever they may be described as, the politics of the United Nations cannot be fitted into the framework of liberal democracy, except as a figure of speech. Whether those of the European Union as a whole can, remains to be seen. This is a fairly substantial reservation.

The second throws doubt on the widely held – indeed, in American public discourse universally held – proposition that liberal-democratic government is always and *ipso facto* superior or at least preferable to non-democratic government. No doubt this is true, other things being equal, but other things sometimes are not. I will not ask you to consider the case of the impoverished Ukraine, which has acquired democratic politics (more or less) at the price of losing two thirds of the modest national product that state had in Soviet times. Look rather at Colombia, a republic which by Latin American standards – indeed, by the criteria generally accepted today – has an almost unique record of virtually continuous constitutional representative democratic government. Two rival electoral parties, Liberals and Conservatives, have generally been in political competition as the theory requires. Colombia has never been under the rule of the military or of populist caudillos for more than brief moments. And yet, although the country has not been involved in international wars, the number of people killed, maimed and driven from their homes in Colombia over the past half-century runs into millions. Almost certainly it far exceeds that in any other country of the western hemisphere. It is certainly larger than in any of the countries of that continent notoriously plagued with military dictatorships. I am not suggesting that non-democratic regimes are better than democratic regimes. I merely remind you of the fact, which is too often overlooked, that the well-being of countries does not depend on the presence or absence of any single brand of institutional arrangement, however morally commendable.

The third observation was expressed in Winston Churchill's classical saying, 'Democracy is the worst of all governments, except for all the others.' While this is usually taken to be an argument *for* representative liberal democracy, it is in fact an expression of deep scepticism. Whatever the campaign rhetoric, political analysts and practitioners remain extremely sceptical of representative mass democracy as an effective way of running governments, or anything else. The case for democracy is essentially negative. Even as an alternative to other systems, it can be defended only with a sigh. This did not matter too much during most of the twentieth century, since the political systems which challenged it – until the end of the Second World War from both the authoritarian right and left, until the end of the Cold War primarily from the authoritarian left – were, or at least to most liberals seemed, so patently awful. Until it faced such a challenge, the built-in defects of liberal representative democracy as a system of government were evident to most serious thinkers as well as to satirists. Indeed, they were widely and frankly discussed even among politicians, until it became inadvisable to say in public what they really thought of the mass of voters on whom their election depended. In countries with long-established traditions of representative government, it was accepted not only because the alternative systems seemed so much worse, but also because, unlike in the terrible era of world wars and global economic catastrophe, very few people actually felt the need for an alternative system – particularly in an era of general prosperity, a better life for even the poor, and comprehensive public welfare systems. It is by no means certain that many parts of the globe now nominally under representative government live in such happy times.

It is, it always was, child's play to criticise the campaign rhetoric of liberal democracy as government. Yet one thing about it is undeniable: 'the people' (whatever group of humans is defined as such) is today the foundation and common point of reference of all state governments except the theocratic. And this is not only unavoidable but right, for if government has any purpose, it must be to speak in the name of and care for the well-being of all citizens. In the age of the common man, all government is government of the people and for the people, though patently it cannot in any operational sense be government *by* the people. This was common ground to liberal democrats, communists, fascists and nationalists of all kinds, even though their ideas differed about how to formulate, express and influence 'the people's will'. It is the common heritage the twentieth century, that century of total wars and co-ordinated economies, has left to the twenty-first. It rests not only on the egalitarianism of peoples no longer willing to accept inferiority in a hierarchical society ruled by 'natural' superiors, but also on the fact that up to now modern national states, economies and social systems could not work without the passive support and even the active participation and mobilisation of very large numbers of their citizens. Mass propaganda was an essential element even of the regimes ready to apply unlimited coercion to their peoples. Even dictatorships cannot long outlast the loss of their subjects' willingness to accept the regime. That is why, when it came to the point, the so-called 'totalitarian' regimes of eastern Europe – their state apparatus loyal, their machinery of repression in good working order – went quickly and quietly.

It is the heritage of the twentieth century. Will it still be the basis of popular, including liberal-democratic, government in the twenty-first? The argument of this lecture is that the current phase of globalised capitalist development is undermining it, and that this will have, and is already having, serious implications for liberal democracy, as it is at present understood. For democratic politics today rests on two assumptions, one moral – or if you prefer, theoretical – the other practical. Morally speaking, it requires the express support of the regime by the bulk of the citizens, who are presumed to constitute the bulk of the inhabitants of the state. However democratic the arrangements for whites in apartheid South Africa, a regime that permanently disenfranchised most of its population cannot be regarded as democratic. The acts of expressing one's assent to the legitimacy of the political system, such as voting periodically in elections, may be little more than symbolic. Indeed it has long been a commonplace among political scientists that in states with mass citizenship only a modest minority participates constantly and actively in the affairs of their state or mass organisation. This is convenient for those who lead, and indeed, moderate politicians and thinkers have long hoped for a degree of political apathy.[2] But these acts are important. We are today faced with a very obvious secession of citizens from the sphere of politics. Participation in elections seems to be falling in most liberal-democratic countries. If popular election is the primary criterion of representative democracy, then how far is it possible to speak of the democratic legitimacy of an authority elected by one third of the potential electorate (the US House of Representatives) or, as in the case of recent British local government and European parliamentary elections, by something like 10 or 20 per cent of the electorate? Or, indeed, of a US president elected by little more than half of the 50 per cent of the Americans entitled to vote?

On the practical side, the governments of modern territorial or nation-states – any government – rest on three presumptions: first, that they have more power than other units operating on their territory; second, that the inhabitants of their territories accept their authority more or less willingly; and third, that governments can provide services for them which could not otherwise be provided equally effectively or at all, such as, in the proverbial phrase, 'law and order'. In the past thirty or forty years these presumptions have increasingly ceased to be valid.

First, while it is still far stronger than any domestic rival, as the past thirty years in Northern Ireland have shown, even the strongest, stablest, most effective states have lost the absolute monopoly of coercive force, not least thanks to the flood of new, small, portable instruments of destruction, now easily accessible to small dissident groups, and the extreme vulnerability of modern life to sudden disruption, however slight. Second, the two strongest pillars of stable government have begun to shake, namely (in countries with popular legitimacy) the voluntary loyalty and service of citizens to states, and (in countries without it) the readiness to obey overwhelming and established state power. Without the first, the total wars based on universal service and national mobilisation would have been as impossible as the rise of the revenue of states to its present share of their GNPs, which, I may remind you, may today top 40 per cent in some countries and is 20 per cent or so even in the US and Switzerland. Without the second, as the history of Africa and large regions of Asia shows, small groups of Europeans could not have maintained colonial rule for generations at relatively modest cost.

The third presumption has been undermined not only by the weakening of state power but, since the 1970s, by a return among politicians and ideologists to an ultra-radical laissez-faire critique of the state which holds that the role of the state must be diminished at all costs. It is argued, with more theological conviction than historical evidence, that any services public authorities can provide are either undesirable or better and more efficiently and cheaply supplied by 'the market'. Since then, the substitution of private or privatised services for public services (and, incidentally, also for co-operative services) has been massive. Such characteristic activities of national or local government as post offices, prisons, schools, water supplies and even welfare services have been handed to or transformed into business enterprises; public employees have been transferred to independent agencies or replaced by commercial subcontractors. Even parts of warfare have been subcontracted. And, of course, the modus operandi of the profit-maximising private firm has become the model to which even government aspires. And to the extent that this happens, the state tends to rely on private economic mechanisms to replace the active and passive mobilisation of its citizens. At the same time, it cannot be denied that in the rich countries of the world the extraordinary triumphs of the economy put more at the disposal of most consumers than government or collective action had ever promised or provided in poorer times.

But here precisely lies the problem. The ideal of market sovereignty is not a complement to liberal democracy, but an alternative to it. Indeed, it is an alternative to any kind of politics, since it denies the need for political decisions, which are precisely decisions about common or group interests as distinct from the sum of choices, rational or otherwise, of individuals pursuing their private preferences. In any case, it holds that the continuous discriminating process of discovering what people want, which the market (and market research) provides, must be more efficient than the occasional recourse to crude electoral head-counting. Participation in the market replaces participation in politics; the consumer takes the place of the citizen. Mr Fukuyama has indeed argued that choosing not to vote, like choosing to shop at a supermarket instead of a small local shop, 'reflects a democratic choice that populations make. They *want* consumer sovereignty.'[3] No doubt they do, but is this choice compatible with what has been regarded as a liberal-democratic political system?

So the sovereign territorial state or state combination, which is the essential framework of democratic or any other politics, is today weaker than before. The scope and effectiveness of its activities are less than before. Its command over the passive obedience and the active service of its subjects or citizens is declining. Two and a half centuries of unbroken growth in the power, scope, ambitions and capacity to mobilise the inhabitants of modern territorial states, whatever the nature or ideology of their regimes, appear to be at an end. The territorial integrity of modern states – what the French call 'the republic one and indivisible' – is no longer taken for granted. In thirty years, will there be a single Spain, or Italy, or Great Britain, the primary centre of loyalty of its citizens? For the first time in a century and a half this question can realistically be asked. And all this cannot but affect the prospects of democracy.

In the first place, the relationship between citizens and public authorities becomes more remote, and their links more attenuated. There has been a steep decline in that 'divinity that doth hedge' not only Shakespearean kings, but the public symbols of national cohesion and citizen loyalty in any legitimate government, especially democratic ones: the presidency, the monarchy, and, perhaps most dramatically in Britain, Parliament. What could be more significant of its decline than the mere fact that the official visual image of Parliament on our screens is one that barely attempts to conceal a scattering of figures in a space of empty green benches? Its proceedings are no longer reported, even in broadsheets, except as stage confrontation or comic relief. There has been a steep decline in the great political movements or machines for mobilising the poor collectively, which actually gave some real meaning to the word 'democracy'.

Hence there has been a decline in the willingness of citizens to participate in politics, but also in the effectiveness of the classic, and according to conventional theory, the only legitimate way of exercising citizenship, namely the election by universal suffrage of those who represent 'the people' and are therefore authorised to govern on its behalf. Between elections – that is to say, usually for several years – democracy exists only as a potential threat to their or their party's re-election. But this is plainly unrealistic, both from the point of view of citizens and of government. Hence the increasing intellectual shoddiness of the public rhetoric of democratic politicians, especially when confronted with two elements in the actual process of democratic politics which have become increasingly central: the role of the modern media, and the expression of public opinion by direct action (or inaction).

For these are the engines by which some control is exercised over the actions of government between elections. Their development also compensates for the decline in citizen participation, and in the effectiveness of the traditional process of representative government. Headlines, or rather irresistible television images, are the immediate objective of all political campaigns, because they are far more effective than mobilising tens of thousands. And, of course, much easier. The days are long past when all work in a minister's office was put aside to answer an impending critical Parliamentary Question. It is the prospect of publication by an investigative journalist that brings even Number 10 up short. And it is neither parliamentary debates nor even editorial policies which bring about the expressions of public discontent so patent that even governments with the safest majorities have to take notice of them between elections – as over the poll tax, the petrol tax, and the dislike of GM foods. And when they happen, it is quite pointless to dismiss them as the work of small, unelected and untypical minorities, though they usually are.

The central role of mass media in modern politics is patent. Thanks to them, public opinion is more powerful than ever, which explains the uninterrupted rise of the professions that specialise in influencing it. What is less understood is the crucial link between media politics and direct action, that is to say action from below that influences the top decision-makers directly, bypassing the intermediate mechanisms of official representative government. This is most obvious where no such intermediate mechanisms exist – in transnational affairs. We are all familiar with the so-called CNN effect: the politically powerful but totally unstructured feeling that 'something must be done' about those awful atrocity pictures on television – in Kurdistan, in Timor, or wherever – and which has been so strong as to produce some more or less improvised action by governments in response. More recently, the demonstrations in Seattle and Prague have shown the effectiveness of well-targeted direct action by small camera-conscious groups, even on organisations constructed to be immune to democratic political processes, such as the IMF and the World Bank. If there are today headlines such as 'World Financial Leaders Heed Warnings',[4] it is due at least in part to those photogenic punch-ups between bunches of toughs in black balaclavas and riot policemen helmeted and shielded as in medieval battles in the most headline-worthy places.

All this faces liberal democracy with perhaps its most immediate and serious problem. In an increasingly globalised, transnational world, national governments coexist with forces that have at least as much impact on the everyday lives of their citizens as they have, but are to varying extents beyond their control. Yet they do not have the political option of abdicating before the forces outside their control, even if they wanted to. Declarations of impotence about the secular trend of oil prices are not policies, because when something goes wrong, it is the not unfounded conviction of citizens, including business executives, that government can and should do something about it, even in countries such as Italy, where little or nothing is expected from the state, and the US, where large parts of the electorate do not believe in the state. That, after all, is what government is there for.

But what can and should governments do? More than in the past, they are under unceasing pressure from a continuously monitored mass opinion, and they are sensitive to it. This constrains their choices. Nevertheless, governments cannot stop governing. Indeed, they are urged by their PR experts that they must constantly be *seen* to be governing, and this, as we know from late twentieth-century British history, multiplies gestures, announcements, and sometimes unnecessary legislation. However, even without the PR imperative, and contrary to the dreamers of a world ruled entirely (and beneficently) by Adam Smith's 'hidden hand', public authorities are today constantly faced with taking decisions about common interests which are technical as well as political. And here democratic votes (or consumers' choice in the market) are no guide at all. At most they are an accelerator or a brake. The environmental consequences of the unlimited growth of motor traffic and the best ways of dealing with them cannot be discovered simply by referenda. Moreover, these ways may prove to be unpopular, and in a democracy it is unwise to tell the electorate what it does not want to hear. How can the finances of state be rationally organised if governments have convinced themselves that any proposal to raise taxes anywhere amounts to electoral suicide, when election campaigns are therefore contests in fiscal perjury, and government budgets are exercises in fiscal obfuscation? In short, the 'will of the people', however expressed, cannot actually determine the specific tasks of government. As those neglected theorists of democracy Sidney and Beatrice Webb observed apropos of trade unions, it cannot judge projects, only results. It is immeasurably better at voting against than for. And when it has actually achieved one of its major negative triumphs, such as toppling the fifty years of corrupt post-war regimes in Italy and Japan, it is unable by itself to supply an alternative. We shall see whether it can do so in Serbia.

And yet, government is for people. Its effects are to be judged by what it does to people. However uninformed, ignorant or even stupid the 'will of the people' is, however inadequate the methods for discovering it, it is indispensable. How else can we assess the way techno-political solutions for problems concerning humanity, however expert and technically satisfactory in other respects, affect the lives of real human beings? Soviet systems failed because there was no two-way traffic between those who took decisions 'in the interests of the people' and those on whom these decisions were imposed. The laissez-faire globalisation of the past twenty years has made the same mistake. It was the work of governments that systematically removed all obstacles to it, on the advice of the most authoritative of technically expert economists. After twenty years of failing to pay attention to the social and human consequences of unfettered global capitalism, the president of the World Bank has come to the conclusion that for most of the world's population the word 'globalisation' suggests 'fear and insecurity' rather than 'opportunity and inclusion'.[5] Even Alan Greenspan and US Treasury Secretary Larry Summers agree that 'antipathy to globalisation runs so deep' that 'a retreat from market-oriented policies and a return to protectionism' are real possibilities.

Still, there is no denying that under liberal democracy listening to the will of the people makes government more difficult. The ideal solution is now hardly ever available to governments. It is the one on which the medical profession and air pilots relied in the past, and still try to rely on in an increasingly suspicious world, namely the popular conviction that we and they share the same interests. We did not tell them how to serve us, since as non-experts we could not, but until something went wrong we gave them our confidence. Few governments, as distinct from political regimes, today enjoy this fundamental a priori confidence. In liberal, i.e. multi-party, democracies they rarely even represent an actual majority of the votes, let alone of the electorate (in the UK, no single party since 1931 has won more than 50 per cent of the vote; nor has any government since the wartime coalition represented a clear majority). The old-style schools and engines of democracy, the mass parties and organisations, which once provided 'their' governments with just such a priori confidence and steady support, have crumbled. In the omnipresent and all-powerful media, backseat drivers, claiming a rival expertise to government, are constantly commenting on government performance.

Under these circumstances, the most convenient, sometimes the only, solution for democratic governments is to keep as much decision-making as possible outside the range of publicity and politics, or at least to sidestep the process of representative government, which means both the ultimate electorate and the activities of assemblies and agencies elected by it. (The US, admittedly an extreme case, only functions as a state with a coherent government policy because presidents have sometimes found ways to bypass the extraordinary antics of the democratically elected Congress.) Even in Britain, the striking centralisation of an already strong decision-making power has gone hand in hand with a demotion of the House of Commons and a massive transfer of functions to unelected institutions, public or private, under both Conservative and Labour governments. A good deal of politics will be negotiated and decided behind the scenes. This will increase the citizens' distrust of government and lower their opinion of politicians. Governments will fight a constant guerrilla war against the coalition of well-organised minority campaigning interests and the media. These will increasingly see as their political function the publication of what governments would prefer to keep quiet, while – such is the irony of a society based on a limitless flow of information and entertainment – they rely on the propagandists of the institutions they should criticise to fill their screens and pages.

So what is the future of liberal democracy in this situation? On paper it does not look too bleak. Except for Islamic theocracy, there are no longer powerful political movements challenging this form of government in principle, and none is likely to arise in the immediate future. The second half of the twentieth century was the golden age of military dictatorships, which were a far greater danger to Western and independent ex-colonial electoral regimes than communism. The twenty-first century does not look quite so favourable to them. None of the numerous ex-communist states has chosen to follow this road, and in any case, almost all such regimes lack the full courage of anti-democratic conviction, and claim only to be the saviours of the constitution until the (unspecified) date of a return to civilian rule. Not that we are seeing the last of governments installed by men in tanks at street corners, especially in the many regions of poverty and social discontent.

Again, whatever it looked like before the economic earthquakes of 1997–8, it is now clear that the utopia of a stateless global laissez-faire market will not arrive. Most of the world's population, and certainly those under liberal-democratic regimes deserving the name, will therefore continue to live in operationally effective states, even though in some unhappy regions state power and administration have virtually disintegrated. The majority of the UN membership will make the best of a newly fashionable political system, or (as in large parts of Latin America) of a system long, but intermittently, familiar. It will not succeed too often, but sometimes it may. Politics will therefore continue. Since we shall continue to live in a populist world where governments must take account of 'the people' and the people cannot live without government, democratic elections will go on. They are today almost universally recognised as giving legitimacy, and incidentally, they provide a convenient way for governments to consult 'the people' without necessarily committing themselves to anything very concrete.

In short, we shall be facing the problems of the twenty-first century with a collection of political mechanisms dramatically ill suited to dealing with them. They are effectively confined within the borders of nation-states, whose numbers are growing, and confront a global world which lies beyond their range of operation. It is not even clear how far they can apply within a vast, heterogeneous territory which does possess a common political framework, like the European Union. They face and compete with a world economy effectively operating through quite different units (transnational firms) to which considerations of political legitimacy and common interest do not apply, and which bypass politics. Above all, they face the fundamental problems of the future of the world in an age when the impact of human action on nature and the globe has become a force of geological proportions. The solution, or mitigation, of these problems will require – it must require – measures for which almost certainly no support will be found by counting votes or measuring consumer preferences. This is not an encouraging prospect either for the long-term prospects of democracy or for those of the globe.

We face the third millennium like the apocryphal Irishman who, when asked for the way to Ballynahinch, pondered and said, 'If I were you, I wouldn't start from here.'

But here is where we are starting from.

7

Spreading Democracy

We are at present engaged in what purports to be a planned reordering of the world by the powerful states. The wars in Iraq and Afghanistan are but one part of a supposedly universal effort to create world order by 'spreading democracy'. This idea is not merely quixotic, it is dangerous. The rhetoric surrounding this crusade implies that the system is applicable in a standardised (Western) form, that it can succeed everywhere, that it can remedy today's transnational dilemmas, and that it can bring peace rather than sow disorder. It cannot.

Democracy is rightly popular. In 1647, the English Levellers broadcast the powerful idea that 'all government is in the free consent of the people'. They meant votes for all. Of course, universal suffrage does not guarantee any particular political result, and elections cannot even ensure their own perpetuation – witness the Weimar Republic. Electoral democracy is also unlikely to produce outcomes convenient to hegemonic or imperial powers. (If the Iraq War had depended on the freely expressed consent of 'the world community', it would not have happened.) But these uncertainties do not diminish the appeal of electoral democracy.

Several other factors besides democracy's popularity explain the dangerous and illusory belief that its propagation by foreign armies may actually be feasible. Globalisation suggests that human affairs are evolving towards a universal pattern. If gas stations, iPods and computer geeks are the same worldwide, why not political institutions? This view underrates the world's complexity. The relapse into bloodshed and anarchy that has occurred so visibly in much of the world has also made the idea of spreading a new order more attractive. The Balkans seemed to show that areas of turmoil and humanitarian catastrophe required the intervention, military if need be, of strong and stable states. In the absence of effective international governance, some humanitarians are still ready to support a world order imposed by US power. But one should always be suspicious when military powers claim to be doing favours for their victims and the world by defeating and occupying weaker states.

Yet another factor may be the most important: the US has been ready with the necessary combination of megalomania and messianism, derived from its revolutionary origins. Today's US is unchallengeable in its techno-military supremacy, convinced of the superiority of its social system, and, since 1989, no longer reminded, as even the greatest conquering empires always were, that its material power has limits. Like President Woodrow Wilson, a spectacular international failure in his day, today's ideologues see a model society already at work in the

US: a combination of law, liberal freedoms, competitive private enterprise, and regular contested elections with universal suffrage. All that remains is to remake the world in the image of this 'free society'.

This idea is dangerous whistling in the dark. Although Great Power action may well have morally or politically desirable consequences, identifying with it is perilous because the logic and methods of state action are not those of universal rights. All established states put their own interests first. If they have the power, and the end is considered sufficiently vital, states justify the means of achieving it (though rarely in public), particularly when they think God is on their side. Both good and evil empires have produced the barbarisation of our era, to which the 'war against terror' has now contributed.

While threatening the integrity of universal values, the campaign to spread democracy will not succeed. The twentieth century demonstrated that states could not simply remake the world or abbreviate historical transformations. Nor can they easily effect social change by transferring institutions across borders. Even within the ranks of territorial nation-states, the conditions for effective democratic government are rare: an existing state enjoying legitimacy, consent, and the ability to mediate conflicts between domestic groups. Without such consensus there is no single sovereign 'people' and therefore no legitimacy for arithmetical majorities. When this consensus – be it religious, ethnic, or both – is absent, democracy has been suspended (as is the case with democratic institutions in Northern Ireland), the state has split (as in Czechoslovakia), or society has descended into permanent civil war (as in Sri

Lanka). 'Spreading democracy' aggravated ethnic conflict and produced the disintegration of states in multinational and multi-communal regions after both 1918 and 1989, a bleak prospect.

Beyond its scant chance of success, the effort to spread standardised Western democracy also suffers from a fundamental paradox. In no small part, it is conceived of as a solution to the dangerous transnational problems of our day. A growing part of human life now occurs beyond the influence of voters, in transnational public and private entities that have no electorates, or at least no democratic ones. And electoral democracy cannot function effectively outside political units such as nation-states. The powerful states are therefore trying to spread a system that even they find inadequate to meet today's challenges.

Europe proves the point. A body like the European Union could develop into a powerful and effective structure precisely because it has no electorate other than a small number (albeit growing) of member governments. The EU would be nowhere without its 'democratic deficit', and there can be no future for its parliament for there is no 'European people', only a collection of 'member peoples' less than half of whom bothered to vote in the 2004 EU parliamentary elections. 'Europe' is now a functioning entity, but unlike the member-states it enjoys no popular legitimacy or electoral authority. Unsurprisingly, problems arose as soon as the EU moved beyond negotiations between governments and became the subject of democratic campaigning in the member-states. Democracy, however desirable, is not an effective device for solving global or transnational problems.

The effort to spread democracy is also dangerous in a more indirect way: it conveys to those who do not enjoy this form of government the illusion that it actually governs those who do. But does it? We now know something about how the actual decisions to go to war in Iraq were taken in at least two states of unquestionable democratic bona fides, the US and the UK. Other than creating complex problems of deceit and concealment, electoral democracy and representative assemblies had little to do with that process. Decisions were taken among small groups of people in private – not very different from the way they would have been taken in non-democratic countries. Fortunately, media independence could not be easily circumvented in the UK. But it is not electoral democracy that necessarily ensures the effective freedom of the press, citizen rights, and an independent judiciary.

8

Terror

Did the nature of political terror change in the late twentieth century? Let me begin with the unexpected rise of violence in a hitherto peaceful island, Sri Lanka, shared by a majority of Buddhist Sinhalese (whose religion and ideology are about as averse to violence as can be) and a minority of Tamils who migrated from south India centuries ago or came as plantation labourers in the late nineteenth century (their Hinduism is not conducive to violence either). The anti-imperialist movement in Sri Lanka was neither very militant nor strikingly effective, and the country got its freedom quietly, in effect as a by-product of Indian independence. Colonial Sri Lanka had indeed developed a smallish Communist Party and, curiously enough, a much larger Trotskyist Party, both led by educated and charming members of the Westernised elite, and both, as good Marxists, opposed to terrorism. There were no attempted insurrections. After independence, the country pursued a quiet, mildly socialist course, which was excellent for the welfare and life expectancy of the population. In short, by Asian standards, Sri Lanka before the 1970s was a rare island of civility, like Costa Rica and (before the 1970s) Uruguay in Latin America. Today, it is running in blood.

The Tamils, a minority of 25 per cent over-represented in the educated professions, developed a comprehensible resentment against a Sinhalese regime which in the 1950s decided to exchange Sinhalese for English as the national administrative language. In the 1970s, a separatist Tamil movement, not without support from a south Indian state, developed armed organisations, the ancestors of today's Liberation Tigers of Tamil Eelam, who have been conducting an effective civil war since the mid-1980s. They are best known as one of the great pioneers and probably the largest operators of suicide bombing – incidentally, since their ideology is secularist, without the usual religious motivations. The Tamils are not quite strong enough to secede, and the Sri Lankan army is too weak to defeat them in military terms. Intransigence on both sides has continued the war in spite of various attempts by third parties (India, Norway) to mediate a settlement.

Meanwhile, two things happened in the majority Sinhalese society. Ethnic-linguistic tensions created a strong Sinhalese backlash that took the form of a nationalist ideology based on Buddhism and racial superiority, since the Sinhalese language is Indo-European ('Aryan'). Curiously enough, this racism is in the tradition of Hindu India, and indeed, in Sri Lanka as in Pakistan, the old Hindu caste system can still be traced under the official egalitarian surface. At the same time, in the early

1970s, the JVP, a leftist body based mainly on educated Sinhalese youth who could not find suitable jobs and on Castroite ideas with a dash of Maoism and a great deal of resentment against the old socio-political elite, organised an important insurrection. It was put down with some toughness and a lot of kids were jailed for a while. Out of the relics of this 1968-type youth rebellion there emerged a militant terrorist organisation based mainly in the Sinhalese countryside and which modulated its original Maoism into a passionate Sinhalese Buddhist-racist chauvinism. In the 1980s it organised a campaign of systematic assassination against political opponents which made high politics a high-risk activity. (The recently retired president of Sri Lanka has seen her father, a former prime minister, and her husband assassinated in front of her eyes, and has lost an eye to similar attempts to murder her.) Terror was also used systematically to establish control in the towns and villages of the countryside.

As in the case of the Maoist Sendero Luminoso movement in the Peru of the 1980s, it is impossible to know how far JVP rule was based on initial mass support, how far that support was alienated by terror, and how far in turn terror is offset by resentment against government repression and generates scepticism about the revolutionaries. Two things are clear. JVP had mass support among sections of the labouring rural Sinhalese population whose educated members provided its cadres, and JVP practised a lot of killing, mostly undertaken by a cadre of what in Latin America would have been called *sicarios*, or mass murderers. The JVP bid for power was put down in the same way, namely by the equivalent of the Latin American 'dirty wars', which aimed at the elimination of rebel leaders and cadres. By the mid-1990s it was estimated that about sixty thousand had fallen victim to these conflicts. The JVP has, since its origins in the late 1960s, moved in and out of official Sri Lankan politics.

It seems evident that Sri Lanka is merely one example of the striking increase in and mutation of political violence in the late twentieth-century world. Another even more prominent one is the rise and theoretical justification of indiscriminate murder as a form of small-group terrorism. With rare exceptions, this practice had been condemned by earlier terrorist movements, and avoided by movements as recent as the Spanish ETA and the Provisional IRA. In the Muslim world, theological justifications – for example, that anyone outside a highly restricted form of orthodoxy could be killed as an 'apostate' – seem to have been revived in the early 1970s by an extremist pre-Al Qaeda secession from the old-established Muslim Brotherhood in Egypt. The fatwa, by Osama bin Laden's religious adviser, formally authorising the killing of innocents was not issued until the end of 1992.[1]

The question 'Why?' is too wide for this essay, not least because it is difficult to disentangle from a general rise in Western societies in the level of socially accepted violence or direct action in image and reality. This has followed a long period when, in most of these societies, civilisation was expected to bring about its permanent decline.

It would be tempting to say that general social violence and political violence have nothing to do with each other, since some of the worst political violence can occur in countries with a notably non-violent political and social tradition, such as Sri

Lanka or Uruguay. Nevertheless, the two cannot be kept apart in countries with a liberal tradition, if only because these are the ones in which unofficial political violence became prominent in the last third of the twentieth century, and so, consequently, did the state's usually greater counter-violence. Dictatorial or authoritarian countries leave little scope for it while they remain in working order, just as they leave hardly any scope for non-violent unofficial politics.

The rise of violence in general is part of the process of barbarisation that has gathered strength in the world since the First World War, and which I have discussed elsewhere. Its progress is particularly striking in the countries of strong and stable states and (in theory) liberal political institutions, in which public discourse and political institutions distinguish only between two mutually exclusive absolutes, 'violence' and 'non-violence'. This was another way of establishing the legitimacy of the national state's monopoly of coercive force, which went hand in hand with the wholesale disarming of the civil population in the nineteenth-century developed states, except in the US, which has therefore always tolerated a higher degree of violence in practice, though not in theory. Since the late 1960s states have lost some of that monopoly of power and resources and more of the sense of legitimacy which made citizens law-abiding. This alone is enough to explain much of the rise in violence.

Liberal rhetoric always failed to recognise that no society operates without *some* violence in politics, even in the quasi-symbolic form of strike-pickets or mass demonstrations, and that violence has gradations and rules, as everyone in societies where it is part of the fabric of social relations knows, and as the

International Red Cross tries constantly to remind the barbarised belligerents of the twenty-first century. The theological or legal casuistry of Al Qaeda or the defenders of 'rendition' is necessary precisely because the accepted rules they break – the Koranic restrictions on killing, and the abhorrence of torture – are so deeply rooted. But when societies or social groups unused to a high degree of social violence find themselves practising it, or when the normal rules break down in traditionally violent societies, the established limits on the use or degree of violence can go. For instance, it is my impression that traditional peasant rebellions, allowing for the general brutality of rural life and behaviour, were not usually very bloodthirsty – generally less so than their suppression. When they went in for massacre or atrocity, it was usually directed against specific persons or categories of persons and property – for instance, houses of the gentry – and conversely others were specifically excepted because they had a good reputation. The violent acts were not arbitrary but, one might almost say, ritually prescribed by the occasion. It was not the 1917 Revolution but the Russian Civil War which brought wholesale massacre to the Russian countryside. But when the brakes on customary behaviour are off, the results can be terrifying. One of the reasons why Colombian narco-gangsters were so successful in the US was, I understand, that in their struggle with rivals they no longer accepted the customary macho convention that one does not kill one's adversary's women and children.

This pathological degeneration of political violence applies to both insurrectionaries and state forces. It is favoured by the growing anomie of inner-city life, especially among the young,

126

and reinforced by the spread of both drug culture and private weaponry. At the same time, the decline of the old conscript national service armies and the rise of a full-time professional soldiery, and particularly of special elite forces such as the SAS, remove the inhibitions of men who remain essentially civilians from the *esprit de corps* of state agents whose exclusive dedication is to the use of force. Meanwhile, there has been a virtual abolition of the conventional limits on what can be shown and described in the increasingly omnipresent and all-enveloping media. The sight, sound and description of violence in its extreme forms are part of everyday life, and the social controls on its practice are consequently diminished. In Soviet Russia, or at least in the cities where there were adequate criminological data, something like 80 to 85 per cent of homicides were committed under the influence of alcohol. We no longer need such a remover of inhibitions.

However, there is a more dangerous producer of unlimited violence. It is the ideological conviction that has dominated both international and internal conflicts since 1914, that one's own cause is so just and the adversary's so terrible that all means to achieve victory or avoid defeat are not only legitimate but necessary. This means that both states and insurrectionaries feel they have a moral justification for barbarism. It was observed in the 1980s that young militants of Sendero Luminoso in Peru were quite ready to kill peasants by the score with a perfectly clear conscience: they were, after all, not acting as individuals who might have feelings in the matter, but as soldiers for the cause.[2] Nor were the army or navy officers training recruits in the techniques of torture on the bodies of political prisoners necessarily brutes and sadists in a private capacity. As in the case of the SS, who were actually punished for private manslaughter as they were trained to commit mass murder calmly,[3] this made their activities more rather than less reprehensible. The rise of mega-terror in the last century reflected not 'the banality of evil' but the substitution of superior imperatives to moral concepts. Nevertheless, at least initially, the immorality of such behaviour may be recognised, as in the military regimes of Latin America, when *all* Argentine officers in a unit might be obliged to take part in torture in order to bond them together in what was recognised as shared infamy. It is to be feared that the acceptance of torture has become too routinised for such gestures in the twenty-first century.

The rise of barbarism has been continuous but uneven. It reached a peak of inhumanity between 1914 and the late 1940s in the era of the two world wars and their revolutionary aftermaths, and of Hitler and Stalin. The Cold War era brought a distinct improvement in the First and Second Worlds, the developed capitalist countries and the Soviet region, but not in the Third World. This does not mean that barbarism actually regressed. In the West it was this period, *c.* 1960 to 1985, which saw the rise of officially trained torturers, and a historically unprecedented wave of military regimes in Latin America and the Mediterranean waging 'dirty wars' on their citizens. Nevertheless, many hoped that after the great change of 1989 the fog of religious wars that had drenched the twentieth century would be dispersed, and with it a major generator of barbarism. Unfortunately, this did not happen. While the sheer scale of human suffering increased dramatically in the 1990s, religious wars fuelled by secular ideologies were reinforced with, or replaced by, a return to various brands of crusading and counter-crusading religious fundamentalism.

Leaving aside the bloodshed and destruction of inter-state or state-sponsored warfare – for example, Vietnam, the indirect superpower confrontations of the 1970s in Africa and Afghanistan, and the Indo-Pakistan and Iraq–Iran wars – there have been three major bouts of political violence and counter-violence since the 1960s. The first was the revival of what had best be called 'neo-Blanquism' in the 1960s and 1970s, namely the attempt by self-selected and generally small elite groups to overthrow regimes or to achieve the objectives of separatist nationalism through armed action. This was largely confined to western Europe, where these groups, primarily of middle-class origin and generally lacking popular support outside universities (except in Northern Ireland), relied largely on media-attracting terrorist actions (the Red Army Fraction in Federal Germany), but also on well-targeted coups capable of destabilising their countries' high politics, such as the assassination of General Franco's presumed successor in 1973 (by ETA) and the kidnapping and murder of the Italian prime minister Aldo Moro in 1978 (by the Red Brigades). In Latin America, such groups chiefly attempted to initiate guerrilla activity and armed operations by larger units, usually in outlying regions, but in some cases (Venezuela, Uruguay) also in cities. Some of these operations were fairly serious: in the three years of the Montonero insurgency in Argentina the regular and irregular forces suffered 1642 casualties (dead and wounded).[4] The limitations of these groups were particularly clear in rural guerrilla warfare, where a substantial degree of popular support is essential not only to success but to survival. The attempts by outsiders to establish guerrilla movements on the Cuban model were spectacularly unsuccessful everywhere in South America, except in Colombia, where large regions of the country were beyond the control of central government administration and forces.

The second, which only came into its own towards the end of the 1980s, and was enormously extended by civil disruption and the collapse of states in the 1990s, is primarily ethnic and confessional. Africa, the western zones of Islam, south and south-east Asia, and south-east Europe were the main regions affected. Latin America remained immune to ethnic and religious conflict, east Asia and the Russian Federation (except for Chechnya) almost unaffected, and the European Union involved only through rising but unbloody xenophobia. Elsewhere, the wave of political violence produced massacre on a scale unknown since the Second World War, and the nearest approach to a revival of systematic genocide. Unlike the European Neo-Blanquists, who usually lacked mass popular support, the activist groups of this period – Al Fatah, Hamas, Palestinian Islamic Jihad, Hezbollah, the Tamil Tigers, the Kurdistan Workers Party, etc. – could rely on the massive support of their constituency, and a source of permanent recruitment. Acts of individual terror were therefore not central to such movements, except as the only available response to the overwhelming military power of the occupying state (as in Palestine), or at best, in civil wars, as a compensation for the vastly superior armaments of the adversary (as in Sri Lanka).

Here, a major innovation of the period was to prove unusually formidable: the suicide bomber. Originally a spin-off from the Iranian Revolution of 1979, carrying its powerful ideology of Shia Islam, and with its idealisation of martyrdom, it was first used to decisive effect in 1983 against the Americans by the Hezbollah in Lebanon. Its effectiveness was so patent that it spread to the Tamil Tigers in 1987, Hamas in Palestine in 1993, and to Al Qaeda and other Islamic ultras in Kashmir and Chechnya between 1998 and 2000.[5] The other most striking development of individual and small-group terrorism in this period was the remarkable revival of political assassination. If 1881 to 1914 was the first golden age of top-level political homicide, the years from the mid-1970s to the mid-1990s became the second: Sadat in Egypt, Rabin in Israel, Rajiv Gandhi and Mrs Gandhi in India, a clutch of leaders in Sri Lanka, Franco's successor-apparent in Spain, prime ministers in Italy and Sweden (though the political element is doubtful in Sweden). There were also attempts on the lives of Pope John Paul II and President Reagan in 1981. The consequences of these actions were not revolutionary, though they sometimes had distinct political effects, as in Israel, Italy and perhaps Spain.

However, the universal reach of television has since made politically more effective actions aimed not at decision-makers but at maximum media impact. After all, such actions ended the formal military presence of the US in Lebanon in the 1980s, in Somalia in the 1990s, and, indeed, in Saudi Arabia after 2001. One of the unhappy signs of barbarisation is the discovery by terrorists that, provided it is within reach of the world's screens, the mass murder of otherwise insignificant men and women has greater headline value than all but the most celebrated or symbolic targets for their bombs.

In the third phase, which appears to dominate at the start of the present century, political violence has become systematically global, both through the policies of the US under President George W. Bush and through the establishment, perhaps for the first time since late nineteenth-century Anarchism, of a terrorist movement consciously operating transnationally. Here, mass popular support once again became irrelevant. The original Al Qaeda appears to have been a structured, elite organisation, but it operated as a decentralised movement in which small, isolated cells were designed to act with no popular backing or direct support whatever. Nor is a territorial base required. It, or a loose network of Islamic cells inspired by it, has thus survived the loss of a base in Afghanistan and the marginalisation of Osama bin Laden's leadership. It is characteristic of this period that civil wars or other conflicts that could not be fitted into the global picture, like the continuing conflicts in Sri Lanka, Nepal and Colombia, or the troubles in the failed or failing states of Africa, raised only intermittent interest in the West.

Two things characterised these new movements. They consisted of small minorities, even when these minorities enjoyed some passive sympathy from the masses in whose name they claimed to act, and their characteristic modus operandi was that of small group action. The so-called 'active service units' of the Provisional IRA are said to have amounted to no more than two or three hundred individuals at any one time, and I doubt whether the Red Brigades in Italy or the Basque ETA were any bigger. The most formidable of the international terrorist movements, Al Qaeda, probably amounted in its Afghan days to no more than four thousand individuals.[6] Their second characteristic was that, with rare exceptions, such as Northern Ireland, 'they are on average more educated and from a higher social background than other members of the community to which they belong'.[7] The prospective Al Qaeda recruits who went to train in Afghanistan in the 1990s are described as 'from the middle and upper class, nearly all from intact families . . . largely college-educated with a strong bias toward the natural sciences and engineering . . . few of them products of religious schools'.[8] Even in Palestine, where they represent a cross-section of the population of the occupied territories including a high proportion from refugee camps, 57 per cent of suicide bombers have some education beyond high school, compared with just 15 per cent of the population of comparable age.[9]

Small though these groups are, they have been formidable enough for governments to mobilise relatively or even absolutely enormous counter-force against them. But here there is an interesting divergence between the First and the Third Worlds (while it lasted, the Second World of communist regimes, though on the verge of collapse, remained entirely immune to such movements until it actually fell to pieces). On the whole, in Europe at least, during the first two of the periods considered here, the new political violence was met with limited force and without major breaks in constitutional governments, although there were moments of hysteria and some serious excesses of power, especially by the state's police and formal or informal armed forces. Was this because the European movements posed no major threat to the national regimes? It is true that they didn't, and still do not, though national separatist movements in Northern Ireland and in the Basque countries have indeed got closer to achieving their ends politically, with the help of the armed pressure of the IRA and ETA. It is also probably true that European police and secret services were and are efficient enough to have infiltrated many of these movements, notably the IRA, and probably the Red Brigades in Italy. Nevertheless, it is significant that in spite of some ruthless counter-terrorism by 'unknown official entities' both in Ireland and in Spain there were no 'dirty wars' on the scale and with the degree of systematic torture and terror that we find in Latin America. Here, the degree of counter-terror far exceeded the political violence of the insurrectionaries, even when these were given to committing atrocities, such as the Senderistas in Peru.

These infamous 'dirty wars' were essentially directed against groups of this kind, and often also undertaken by small forces of professional specialists corresponding to those of the minority terrorists. Thus in Latin America the objective of the torturing regimes, insofar as it was not a pathological degeneration of politics, was not usually to deter people from taking part in subversive activities, but more concretely to get information from activists about their groups. Neither was deterrence the objective of death squads; it was rather to get rid of people they regarded as guilty without legal delays or the risk of acquittals. Terror against entire populations regarded as dissident is usually brutal enough, as in apartheid South Africa and Palestine, but more rough and ready. The number of people killed in Palestine before the second Intifada was almost certainly lower than the number of those 'disappeared' in Pinochet's Chile. Admittedly barbarisation has progressed far enough for repression which produces only a corpse or two per day to be considered as below the level of massacre that automatically reaches the headlines. Even so, the authorities in countries such as Colombia and Peru have fought their rural guerrilla movements with unusual ferocity.

The globalisation of the 'war against terror' since September 2001 and the revival of armed foreign intervention by a major power which formally denounced the hitherto accepted rules and conventions of international conflict in 2002 has transformed the situation for the worse. The actual danger of the new international terrorist networks to the regimes of stable states in the developed world, but also in Asia, remains negligible. A few score or a few hundred victims of bombs on metropolitan transport systems in London or Madrid hardly disrupt the operational capacity of a big city for more than a matter of hours. Horrifying though the carnage of 9/11 was in New York, it left the international power of the US and its internal structures completely unaffected. If things have changed for the worse, it is not by the action of the terrorists but by those of the US government. India, the world's largest democracy, is a good example of the capacity of a stable state to resist. Though in the last twenty years it has lost two leaders to assassins, and it lives with a situation of low-level war in Kashmir, a wide selection of guerrilla movements in its north-eastern provinces, and Marxist-Leninist (Naxalite) insurgency in some tribal areas, nobody would dream of suggesting that it remains other than a stable state in full operational order.

This underlines the relative and absolute weakness of the current phase of terrorist movements. They are symptoms, not significant historic agents. This is not altered by the fact that thanks to changes in armaments and tactics small groups and even individuals can do far more damage per capita than they used to, or by the utopian aims held by or ascribed to some terrorist groups. Operating in stable states with stable regimes, and without the support of material sectors of the population, they are a police and not a military problem. Even when small-group terrorism is part of a general movement of dissidence, as the offshoots of Al Qaeda are in the Iraq resistance, they are not the main or militarily effective part of the movement, but only marginal additions to it. As for operating outside the range of a sympathetic population, such as Palestinian suicide bombers in Israel or a handful of young Muslim fanatics in London, they have little more than propaganda value. None of this means that major international police measures are not needed to fight small-group terrorism, especially the transnational type, if only because there is a danger that at some time in the future such groups may manage to acquire a nuclear device and the ability to use it. Their political potential, mainly destructive, in unstable or decomposing states, particularly in the Muslim world west of India, is clearly much greater, but should not be confused with the political potential of mass religious mobilisation.

It is comprehensible that such movements create great nervousness among ordinary people, notably in large Western cities, especially when both government and media unite to create a climate of fear for their own purposes by giving them maximum publicity (it is difficult to remember that before 2001 the standard and entirely rational approach of governments faced with such movements – ETA, Red Brigades, IRA – was to 'deprive them of the oxygen of publicity' so far as possible). It is a climate of irrational fear. The current policy of the US has tried to revive the apocalyptic terrors of the Cold War, when they no longer have any plausibility, by inventing 'enemies' that legitimise the expansion and use of its global power. I repeat, the dangers of the 'war against terror' do not come from Muslim suicide bombers.

None of this diminishes the scale of the genuine global crisis of which the transformations of political violence are expressions. They seem to reflect the profound social dislocations brought about at all levels of society by the most rapid and dramatic trans-formation in human life and society ever experienced within single lifetimes. They also seem to reflect both a crisis in tradi-tional systems of authority, hegemony and legitimacy in the west and their breakdown in the east and south, as well as a crisis in the traditional movements that claimed to provide an alter-native to these. They have been exacerbated by the failures of decolonisation in parts of the world and the end of a stable, or indeed any, international system since the collapse of the USSR. And they will prove to be beyond the power of the neo-conservative and neo-liberal utopians of a world of Western liberal values spread by market growth and military interventions.

9

Public Order in an Age of Violence

Some time in the 1970s, the Association of Chief Police Officers told the UK government that it was no longer possible to prevent public disorder in the streets as in the past without a new Public Order Act. A few years later, in the early 1980s I suppose, I was invited to a colloquium somewhere in Norway, and I noted that the booking pamphlet for the hotel at which it was to be held – the usual convention centre in some tourist landscape – advertised that the hotel had guaranteed bullet-proof windows. In Norway? Yes, in Norway. Let me begin this lecture with these two incidents. The age has become more violent, including its images. There is no doubt about it. My lecture is about what this means, and how governments should set about protecting the ordinary life of their citizens. It is primarily about Britain, where the rise in public violence (as shown in the crime figures) is particularly striking. However, the problem does not concern only one country. Nor is it just about terrorism.

The subject is much bigger than that. For instance, it includes football hooliganism, another historically novel phenomenon that came into its own in the 1970s.

Patently, as my Norwegian recollection suggests, a lot of this violence is made possible by the extraordinary explosion in the global supply and availability to private persons and groups of sufficiently cheap, powerfully destructive arma- ments capable of being handled by anybody. This was originally the result of the Cold War, but since a lot of money is to be made from these devices, production has continued to soar. Every decade since 1960 has seen the number of firms producing them rise, especially in western Europe and North America. In 1994 there were three hundred companies in fifty-two countries in the small-arms business, 25 per cent more than in the mid-1980s; in 2001 the number was esti- mated at five hundred. To put it another way: Kalashnikovs, or AK47 assault rifles, originally developed in the Soviet Union during the Second World War, are a most formidable form of small arms, and according to the *Bulletin of Atomic Scientists*, anything up to 125 million of them are circulating in the world today. You can order them on the Internet, at least in the US, at Kalashnikov USA. As for handguns and knives, who can count them?

But, of course, public disorder, even in the extreme form of terrorism, does not depend on high-tech or expensive equip- ment, as was demonstrated on 11 September 2001. The hijackers of the planes that brought down the Twin Towers were armed only with carpet-cutters. The most long-lasting armed groups, such as the IRA and ETA, relied primarily on explosives, some of which could actually be home-produced. The 7 July bombers in the UK produced their own. If recent reports are correct, the entire massacre of 7/7 cost the bombers only a few hundred pounds. Plus, of course, their lives. So, while not forgetting that the world today is more awash with things that kill and maim than ever before, that's only one element of the problem.

Is public order harder to maintain? Plainly governments and businesses think so. The size of police forces in Britain has gone up by 35 per cent since 1971; and for every ten thousand citizens at the end of the century there were thirty-four police officers as against 24.4 thirty years earlier (that's more than 40 per cent up). And I am not even counting the estimated half a million employed in the security industry as guards and the like – a sector of the economy that has multiplied over the past thirty years since Securicor felt big enough in 1971 to get a Stock Exchange quotation. There were about 2500 firms in the industry last year. As you know, the de-industrialisation of Britain has produced a large number of able-bodied men for whom getting a job as a security guard is one of the few available forms of employment. One might say that the economy, instead of being based on taking in one another's washing, may one day rest on the mass employment of people taking on one another's watching.

Not only is more manpower brought into action, but more force. Crowd control specialists nowadays count on four main types of device to deal with troublesome demonstrations: chemicals (e.g. tear gas), 'kinetics' such as riot guns and rubber bullets, water cannon, and stun technology. Here's a list of countries that illustrates the range, from traditional to modern, hard-core crowd control: Norway uses none of the four; Finland, the Netherlands, India and Italy only one, namely chemicals; Denmark, Ireland, Russia, Spain, Canada and Australia use two; and Belgium and the real heavies – the US, Germany, France, the UK plus little Austria – have all four ready for action. Clearly Britain, which once prided itself that its police went completely unarmed, no longer lives in the orderly world of Norway or Finland.

How have these developments come about? I think two things have been happening. The first is the reversal of what Norbert Elias analysed in a work called *The Process of Civilization*, The transformation of public behaviour in the West from the Middle Ages on. It became less violent, more 'polite', more considerate, first within a restricted elite, then on a larger scale. But this is no longer true today. We have become so used to such things as swearing in public, the use of deliberately crude and offensive language, that it is hard to remember how comparatively recent this is. Fucking and blinding had, of course, long been common in groups of males, such as soldiers, specialising in tough activities, although I don't think any Western army has the full range of obscenity of the Russians. Still, when I left the army after the last war, where I had first come across this practice, I still returned to a politer world. Women scarcely used this sort of language, and as a general social practice it started only in the 1960s. That, you may remember, was the decade when the word 'fuck' entered general British print culture. It first appeared in a British dictionary in 1965, and in an American one in 1969.[1]

At the same time, traditional social rules and conventions weakened. For instance, it seems clear that juvenile (between fourteen and twenty years old) delinquency began its dispro-portionate rise in the second half of the 1960s. Young men fuelled by testosterone and male assertion have always been rowdy, especially when organised in groups, something that was ideally kept within limits by tolerating it on special occasions. This applied even to the well-bred young members of P.G. Wodehouse's Drones Club. If you remember, their propensity to knock helmets off coppers on Boat Race Nights got Bertie Wooster into Vine Street nick. But it is not only the erosion of social rules and conventions but of conventions and relations within the family that has turned young men into what the Victorians would have called 'the dangerous classes'. I shan't say more about this, or about the more long-term twentieth-century process of barbarisation which has led to the scandalous situation where Western ideologists actually provide an intel-lectual justification of torture, but of course it is there in the background.

The second, more direct phenomenon also began in the late 1960s. It is the crisis in the sort of state in which we all got used to living in the last century – the territorial nation-state. For 250 years before that turning-point the state kept increas-ing its power, its resources, its range of activities, and its knowledge and control over what happened on its territory. This development was independent of politics and ideology: it happened in liberal, conservative, communist and fascist states. It reached its peak in the golden decades of the welfare state and the mixed economy after the Second World War. But all this was based on the prior assertion of its monopoly of state law and state courts over other laws (e.g. religious law or customary law). The same is true of its monopoly of armed force. In the course of the nineteenth century most Western states eliminated the carrying and use of arms by all citizens except its own agents (except for sport), even in the end the duels of the nobility and gentry. (The US is quite exceptional in this respect, among industrialised countries, as it is in a rising rate of homicide over the past two centuries as against a declining one in Europe.)[2] In Britain, convention even banned the use of knives and daggers in private fights as 'un-English', and rules for fist-fights – the Queensberry Rules – were introduced. In conditions of social stability even official power went disarmed in public. In the UK, policemen were armed only in Ireland, known to be potentially insurrectionary, but not in mainland Britain. Public revolts, riots and marches were institutionalised, that is to say reduced to demonstrations, increasingly by prior negotiation with the police. London's mayor Ken Livingstone has just reminded the Chinese that this is what has happened in both Hyde Park and Trafalgar Square since Victorian days. This was true even in countries we regard as having a penchant for street violence, such as France, whatever the incendiary slogans of mass demonstration.[3] That is why the great Paris student revolt of 1968 produced practically no casualties, on either side. The same is true of the recent mobilisations that defeated the new French youth employment law.

But there is another element in this weakening of the state: the citizens' loyalty to the state and their readiness to do what the state wants them to do are eroding. The two world wars were fought by the belligerents with conscript armies, that is to say with citizen soldiers who were prepared to kill and die by the million 'for their country', as the phrase has it. This is no longer so. I doubt whether any government that gave their citizens some choice in the matter, and several that don't, could do it any longer – certainly not the US, which abolished general military service after the Vietnam War. But in a milder way this also applies to the citizens' readiness to abide by the law, that is to say their sense of the law's moral justification. If we feel a law is legitimate, it is fairly readily obeyed. We believe that football matches rightly require referees and linesmen, and we trust them to exercise their legitimate functions. If we didn't, how much force would be needed to establish and maintain order on the pitch? Many motorists do not accept the moral justification of speed cameras and therefore have no hesitation in avoiding them. If you can get away with smuggling, nobody thinks the worse of you. Once the law lacks legitimacy and abiding by it depends mainly on fear of being caught and punished, it is that much harder to maintain, not to mention more expensive. I think there is little doubt that today, for a variety of reasons, citizens are less likely to abide by the law or by informal conventions of social behaviour than used to be the case.

Furthermore, globalisation, the vast increase in mobility and the large-scale removal of effective frontier controls in Europe and elsewhere have made it increasingly hard for governments to control what comes in and out of their territory, or occurs on it. Thus it is technically impossible to control more than a tiny fraction of the content of containers that come into or go out of our ports without bringing the rhythm of everyday economic life almost to a halt. Illicit traders and traffickers are making full use of this facility, as they have of the inability of states to control or even monitor international financial transactions. The most recent study of this phenomenon, Moisés Naím's book *Illicit*, says flatly, and I quote, 'In the fight against global illicit trade governments are failing . . . There is simply nothing in the cards that points to an imminent reversal of fortune for the myriad networks . . . in illicit trade.'

All this has severely reduced the powers of states and governments in the past thirty years. In extreme cases they may lose control of part of their territories. In 2004 the CIA identified fifty regions around the world over which central governments exert little or no control. 'But,' if I may quote Sr Naím's book on the illegal economy again, 'in fact it is rare today to find a country without pockets of lawlessness that are well integrated into larger global networks.'[4] In less extreme cases it is possible for otherwise stable and flourishing states such as the UK and Spain to live for decades with small armed groups on their territories which their governments are unable to eliminate totally. And this in spite of the evident fact that our information about country and population is far greater than ever before. Although the technological ability of public authorities to keep an eye on their inhabitants, listen in on their conversations, read their emails and, in Britain, watch them through innumerable CCTV cameras is greater today than any government's in the past, they may well know less than their predecessors about the identities and number of people actually on their territory at any moment, where they are living and what they are doing. People who organise censuses today are far less confident about their information than they used to be in the days of George V and George VI – and with good reason.

All this explains why even effective states in good working order have to some extent adjusted to a much higher degree of unofficial violence than in the past. Think of Northern Ireland in the last thirty years. Thanks to a combination of force and tacit arrangements, effective government and normal life, including movement in and out of the province, went on in spite of a situation of sub-civil war. All over the world the rich adjust to the threat of the violent poor by establishing their gated communities, which in Britain are a fairly recent phenomenon, and most obvious in the Docklands. There are said to be a hundred in England, mostly small, though this is nothing compared to the seven million families who live in such fortress compounds in the US, more than half of them in communities 'where access is controlled by gates, entry-codes, key cards and security guards'.[5] As times become more violent, this trend is rising rapidly, as anyone who has been to Rio de Janeiro or Mexico City over the years can confirm. But can anything be done to control the situation?

Two questions arise. First, can the new problems of public order in an age of violence be controlled? The answer must be yes, though to what extent is not yet clear. Football hooliganism is an example of how this can be done. It emerged as a regular mass phenomenon in Britain in the 1960s, and was widely copied in other countries. It reached a peak in the 1980s with the appalling incidents of Bradford and the thirty-nine fatalities at the Heysel Stadium in Brussels during the European Cup final between Liverpool and Juventus. There was much talk of the need for extreme measures, such as compulsory ID cards, but in fact since then football hooliganism has been much reduced in the UK by more moderate measures. These include technical changes such as all-seater grounds and closed-circuit TV, better intelligence and co-ordination, and more selective police tactics, such as isolating known hooligans instead of the blanket 'containment' of all away fans inside and outside the ground. Furthermore, the police have been better able to concentrate on more serious incidents, because controlling order within the grounds has been passed over to club stewards. All this was more expensive, much more expensive, both in money and manpower. Ten thousand men were needed to police Euro 96 in Britain; I have seen no estimates for the cost in money and manpower of the 2006 World Cup in Germany. But the improvement was achieved without the extreme measures suggested at one time. Again, New York today is a much safer place than it was, as those of us who remember the grubby, genuinely dangerous New York of the 1970s and 1980s will confirm. Insofar as this is due to Mayor Rudy Giuliani, this also was done largely through changes in police tactics (zero tolerance) rather than by adding to the New York cops' already impressive arsenal of weaponry.

This brings me to the second question: what is the balance between force and persuasion or public confidence in controlling public order? Keeping order in an age of violence has been both harder and more dangerous, not least for the increasingly armed and technologised police forces, more often than not operating with equipment designed to repel physical attack and looking like medieval knights with shields and armour. Police are tempted to see themselves as a body of 'guardians' with special professional knowledge, separate from (and ignorantly criticised by) the politicians, the courts and the liberal media. The world today – and not only outside Europe – is full of police and security services convinced that, whatever governments and the media say in public, not the rule of law but force (and, if need be, violence) is what keeps order, and that in this belief they have at least the tacit support of both government and public opinion. In this country, after the tranquil 1950s and 1960s, the initial reaction to the new situation with the IRA, miners' strikes and race riots was to start bashing, to become more confrontational, even quasi-military, even in mainland Britain. Facing terrorists has further encouraged the militarisation of the police. The 'shoot to kill' policy has already created several innocent, and avoidable, victims, such as the Brazilian Jean Charles de Menezes. Fortunately, however, Britain has not yet gone far down the continental road to special armed riot squads, such as the French CRS.

On the other hand, two things are part of basic police wisdom. The first is that policemen are not utopians. They are not trying to eliminate crime totally; it has only to be reduced, controlled, kept out of the civilian population's hair. This keeps coppers sceptical of political crusades, though it may also tempt some into corruption. The second, which is even more relevant, is that the people whose public order is to be protected should not be antagonised while the coppers isolate and pursue 'trouble-makers'. Excessive or overt force, especially against groups, may antagonise, if not the public as a whole, then large groups which are believed to contain a disproportionate number of miscreants: blacks, inner-city teenagers, Asians, or whoever. Doing so will multiply the dangers to public order. A good example of how this can happen was the Notting Hill Carnival riot in the 1970s, which was set off by an excessively indiscriminate police 'stop and search' operation against pickpockets, which the local public saw as a racial attack against blacks. This is a real danger. During the Brixton riot of 1981 there is little doubt that the police regarded all blacks as potential rioters, and exacerbated relations with the locals. Fortunately, during the Northern Ireland troubles the police forces in mainland Britain largely resisted the temptation to regard all Irish people as potential members of the IRA. Maintaining public order, whether in an age of violence or not, depends on a balance between force, confidence and intelligence.

In this country, under normal circumstances, give or take the occasional breakdown, one might, by and large, have confidence in the balance established both by government and the forces of public order. But since 9/11, circumstances have not been normal. We are drowned in a wave of political rhetoric about the unknown but terrible dangers from abroad, the weapons of mass destruction hysteria, the ill-named 'war against terror', and the 'defence of our way of life' against ill-defined external enemies and their terrorist agents within. It is a rhetoric designed to make the flesh of the citizens creep rather than to help fight terror – with what political objectives I leave you to work out. For making the flesh creep or creating panic is precisely what terrorists strive to achieve. Their political objective is not achieved by killing as such, but by publicity for the killing, which demoralises the citizens. During the time when Britain really had a continuous terrorist problem, namely the IRA operations, the fundamental rule of the authorities fighting terror was, if at all possible, not to give them any publicity, or to advertise counter-measures.

So let us clear our mind of this rubbish. The so-called 'war against terror' is not a war except in the metaphorical sense we use when we talk of 'the war against drugs' or 'the war between the sexes'. 'The enemy' is not in a position to defeat us, or even to do us major damage. A recent survey of global terrorism in 2005 by the US State Department lists – omitting Iraq, which is a real war – 7500 'terrorist attacks' worldwide, with 6600 fatalities, which suggests that most such attacks are failures. We are facing small-group terrorists such as we have long been used to, only with two significant innovations. Unlike earlier terrorists, they are ready for, and may indeed aim at, indiscriminate massacre. Indeed, they have achieved one massacre that killed in four figures, a few that killed hundreds, and quite a lot with two-digit fatalities. The other is the frightening historical innovation of the suicide bomber. These innovations are serious enough, especially in the era of the Internet and the general accessibility of small, portable but very destructive devices. I am not denying that this is a more serious threat than earlier terrorisms, and it justifies exceptional efforts by those whose business it is to fight it. But, let me repeat, it is not, and it is not

151

going to turn into, a war. It is basically a very serious problem of public order.

But public security, what people mean by 'law and order', is essentially safeguarded by the institutions and authorities of peacetime civil life, including the police. The institutions of war – i.e. mainly the armed forces – are mobilised only in situations of war and on the most rare of occasions when civilian services break down. Even in situations of partial warfare, as in Northern Ireland, long experience has taught us the political dangers of maintaining public order with soldiers, without a regular police force separate from the army. In spite of all the talk about terrorism, no country of the European Union is at war or is likely to be, nor do any EU countries have a social and political fabric sufficiently fragile to be seriously destabilised by small groups of activists. The current phase of international terrorism is more serious than such movements have been in the past because it is capable of massacre and is deliberately indiscriminate, but not as a political or strategic agent. I would say it is less dangerous than the epidemic of political assassinations since the 1970s, which has attracted no great media attention because it doesn't affect Britain and the US. Even 9/11 did not disrupt New York for more than a few hours, and was dealt with rapidly and efficiently by the normal civilian services.

Terrorism requires special efforts, but it is important not to lose our heads over it. In theory, a country that never quite lost its cool during thirty years of Irish troubles should not lose it now. In practice, the real danger of terrorism lies not in the actual danger from anonymous handfuls of fanatics but from

152

the unreasonable fear their activities provoke, and which today both media and unwise governments encourage. This is one of the major dangers of our time, certainly a greater one than small terrorist groups.

10

The Empire Expands Wider Still and Wider

The present world situation is quite unprecedented. The great global empires that have been seen before, such as the Spanish in the sixteenth and seventeenth centuries, and notably the British in the nineteenth and twentieth centuries, bear little comparison with what we see today in the American empire.

We live in a world so integrated, its ordinary operations are so geared to one another, that there are immediate global consequences to any interruption – SARS, for instance, which within days became a global phenomenon, having started from an unknown source somewhere in China. The disruption of the world transport system, international meetings and institutions, global markets, even whole economies, happened with a speed unthinkable in any previous period.

There is the enormous power of a constantly revolutionised technology in economics and, above all, in military force.

Technology is more decisive in military affairs than ever before. Political power on a global scale today requires the mastery of this technology, combined with an extremely large state. Previously the question of size was not relevant: the Britain that ran the greatest empire of its day was, even by the standards of the time, only a medium-sized state. And in the seventeenth century, Holland, a state of the same order of size as Switzerland, could become a global player. Today it is inconceivable that any state, however rich and technologically advanced, other than a relatively giant one could become a global power.

There is the complex nature of today's politics. Our era is still one of nation-states – the only aspect of globalisation where globalisation does not work. But it is a peculiar kind of state where in virtually every one, the ordinary inhabitants play an important role. In the past the decision-makers ran states with little reference to what the bulk of the population thought. And during the late nineteenth and early twentieth centuries governments could rely on a mobilisation of their people which is in retrospect quite unthinkable. Nevertheless, what the population thinks, or is prepared to do, is nowadays more directed for them than before.

A key novelty of the US's imperial project is that all other great powers and empires knew that they were not the only ones, and none aimed at global domination. None believed itself invulnerable, even if it believed itself to be central to the world – as, for instance, China did, or the Roman empire at its peak. Regional domination was the maximum danger envisaged by the system of international relations under which the world lived until the end of the Cold War. A global reach, which became possible after 1492, should not be confused with global domination.

The British empire in the nineteenth century was the only one that really was global, in the sense that it operated across the entire planet, and to that extent it is a possible precedent for the American empire. In contrast, the Russians in the communist period dreamed too of a world transformed, but they knew well, even at the peak of the power of the Soviet Union, that world domination was beyond them, and, contrary to Cold War rhetoric, they never seriously attempted such domination.

But the differences between the ambitions of today's US and those of Britain a century and more ago are stark. First, the US is a physically vast country with one of the largest populations on the globe, still (unlike the European Union) growing due to almost unlimited immigration. There are differences in style, too. The British empire at its peak occupied and administered one quarter of the globe's surface. The US has never actually practised colonialism except briefly during the international fashion for colonial imperialism at the end of the nineteenth century and the beginning of the twentieth century. The US operated instead with dependent and satellite states, notably in the western hemisphere, in which it had virtually no competitors. Unlike Britain, it developed a policy of armed intervention into these in the twentieth century.

Because the decisive arm of the world empire in those days was the navy, the British empire took over strategically important maritime bases and staging-posts worldwide. This is why from Gibraltar to St Helena to the Falklands, the Union Jack flew and still flies. Outside the Pacific, the US began to need this kind of base only after 1941, but they did it by agreement, with what in those days could genuinely be called a coalition of the willing. Today, the situation is different. The US has become aware of the need directly to control a very large number of military bases, as well as indirectly to continue to control them.

There are important differences in the structure of the domestic state itself and its ideology. The British empire had a British but not a universal purpose, although naturally its propagandists also found more altruistic motives for it. So the abolition of the slave trade was used to justify British naval power, as human rights today are often used to justify American military power. On the other hand, the US, like revolutionary France and revolutionary Russia, is a great power based on a universalist revolution, and therefore believes that the rest of the world should follow its example, or possibly even that it should help liberate the rest of the world. Few things are more dangerous than empires pursuing their own interests in the belief that by doing so they are doing humanity a favour.

The basic difference, however, is that the British empire, although global (and in some senses even more global than the US now as it single-handedly controlled the oceans to an extent to which no other country currently has control of the skies), was not aiming at global power or even military and political land power in regions such as Europe and America. The empire pursued the basic interest of Britain, which was its economic interests, with as little interference as possible. It was always aware of the limitations of Britain's size and resources. After 1918, it was acutely aware of its imperial decline.

But the global empire of Britain, the first industrial nation, worked with the grain of the globalisation the development of the British economy did so much to advance. The British empire was a system of international trade which, as industry developed in Britain, essentially rested on the export of manufactures to less developed countries, and in return, Britain became the major market for the world's primary products. After it ceased to be the workshop of the world, it became the centre of the globe's financial system.

Not so the US economy. It rested on the protection of native industries in its potentially gigantic market against outside competition, and this remains a powerful element in US politics. When US industry became globally dominant, free trade suited it as it had suited the British. But one of the weaknesses of the twenty-first-century American empire is precisely that in the industrialised world of today the US economy is no longer as dominant as it was. What the US imports in vast quantities are manufactures from the rest of the world, and against this the reaction of both business interests and voters remains protectionist. There is a contradiction between the ideology of a world dominated by US-controlled free trade, and the political interests of important elements inside the US who find themselves weakened by this.

One of the few ways in which this weakness can be overcome is the expansion of the arms trade. This is another element of difference between the British and American empires.

Particularly since the Second World War, there has been an extraordinary degree of constant armament in the US in a time of peace that has no precedent in modern history; it may be the reason for the dominance of what President Eisenhower called the Military Industrial Complex. During the Cold War, for forty years both sides spoke and acted as though there was a war on, or a war was about to break out. The British empire reached its zenith in the course of a century (1815 to 1914) without major international wars. Moreover, in spite of the evident disproportion between US and Soviet power, this impetus to the growth of the US arms industry became much stronger even before the Cold War ended, and it has continued ever since.

The Cold War turned the US into the hegemon of the Western world. However, this was as the head of an alliance. There was of course no illusion about relative power. The power was in Washington, not anywhere else. In a way, Europe then recognised the logic of an American world empire, whereas today the US government is reacting to the fact that the American empire and its goals are no longer genuinely accepted. There is no coalition of the willing; in fact, present US policy is more unpopular than that of any other US government has ever been, and probably than that of any other great power.

The Americans led the alliance with a degree of courtesy traditional in international affairs, if only because the Europeans should be in the front line in the fight against the Soviet armies, but they insisted it should be alliance permanently welded to the US by depending on American military technology. They remained consistently opposed to an independent military potential in Europe. The roots of the long-standing friction between the Americans and the French since the days of De Gaulle lie in the French refusal to accept any alliance between states as eternal, and the insistence on maintaining an independent potential for producing high-tech military equipment. However, the alliance was, for all its strains, a real coalition of the willing.

Effectively, the collapse of the USSR left the US as the only superpower, which no other power could or wanted to challenge. The sudden emergence of an extraordinary, ruthless, antagonistic flaunting of US power is thus hard to understand, all the more so since it fits in neither with the long-tested imperial policies developed during the Cold War, nor the interest of the US economy. The policies that have recently prevailed in Washington seem to all outsiders so mad that it is difficult to understand what is really intended. But patently a public assertion of global supremacy by military force is what is in the minds of the people who are at present dominating, or at least half dominating, policy-making in Washington. Its purpose remains unclear.

Is it likely to be successful? The world is too complicated today for any single state to dominate it. And with the exception of its military superiority in high-tech weaponry, the US is relying on diminishing assets, or potentially diminishing assets. Its economy, though large, forms a diminishing share of the global economy. It is vulnerable in the short term as well as in the long term. Imagine, for instance, that tomorrow OPEC decided to put all its bills in euros instead of in dollars.

Although the US retains some political advantages, it has

thrown most of them out of the window over the past eighteen months. There are the minor assets of the sheer importance of American culture's domination of world culture, and of the English language. But the major asset Americans have for imperial projects at the moment is military. The American empire is beyond competition on the military side, and it is likely to remain so within the foreseeable future. That does not mean it will be absolutely decisive just because it is decisive in localised wars. But for practical purposes there is nobody, not even the Chinese, within reach of the technology of the Americans. But here there will need to be some careful consideration on the limits of sheer technological superiority.

Of course Americans theoretically do not aim to occupy the whole world. What they aim to do is to go to war, to leave friendly governments behind them, and go home again. This will not work. In pure military terms, the Iraq War was very successful. But, because it was purely military, it neglected the sheer necessities of what to do if you occupy a country – running it, maintaining it, as, for instance, the British did in the classic colonial model of India. The model 'democracy' Americans want to offer to the world with Iraq is a non-model and irrelevant for this purpose. The belief that the US does not need genuine allies among other states, or genuine popular support in the countries its military can now conquer (but not effectively administer), is fantasy.

The war in Iraq was an example of the sheer frivolity of US decision-making. Iraq was a country that had been defeated by the Americans and refused to lie down. It was a country so weak it could be easily defeated. It happened also to have assets – oil –

but basically the war was an exercise in demonstrating international power. The policy the crazies in Washington are talking about, namely a complete re-formulation of the entire Middle East, makes no sense. If their aim is to overthrow the Saudi kingdom, what are they planning to put in its place? If they are serious about changing the Middle East, we know the one thing they have to do is lean on the Israelis. Bush's father was prepared to do this, but the present incumbent in the White House is not. Instead, his administration has destroyed one of the two guaranteed secular governments in the Middle East, and is about to move against the other, Syria.

The emptiness of the policy is clear from the way the aims have been put forward in public relations terms. Phrases such as 'axis of evil' or 'the road map' are not intended to be policy statements, but soundbites that then accumulate their own policy potential. The sheer overwhelming newspeak that has swamped the world in the last eighteen months is an indication of the absence of real policy. Bush does not do policy, but a stage act. Officials such as Richard Perle and Paul Wolfowitz talk like Rambo in public as in private. All that counts is the overwhelming power of the US. In real terms, they mean that the US can invade anybody that's small enough and where they can win quickly enough. This is not a policy. Nor will it work. The consequences of this for the US are going to be very dangerous. Domestically, the real danger for a country that aims at world control, essentially by military means, is that of militarisation – a danger that has been seriously underestimated.

Internationally, the danger is the destabilising of the world.

The Middle East is just one example of this destabilisation: it's far more unstable now than it was ten years ago, or even five years ago. US policy weakens all the alternative arrangements, formal and informal, for keeping order. In Europe, it has wrecked NATO – not much of a loss; but trying to turn it into a world military police force for the US is a travesty. It has deliberately sabotaged the European Union, and also systematically aims at ruining another of the great world achievements since 1945, prosperous democratic social welfare states. The widely perceived crisis over the credibility of the United Nations is less of a drama than it appears because the UN has never been able to do more than operate marginally because of its total dependence on the Security Council, and the use of the US veto.

How is the world to confront – contain – the US? Some people, believing that they have not the power to confront the US, prefer to join them. More dangerous are those who hate the ideology behind the Pentagon but support the US project on the grounds that, in the course of its advance, it will eliminate some local and regional injustices. This may be called an imperialism of human rights. It has been encouraged by the failure of Europe in the Balkans in the 1990s. The division of opinion over the Iraq War showed there was a minority of influential intellectuals, including Michael Ignatieff in the US and Bernard Kouchner in France, who were prepared to back US intervention because they believe it is necessary to have a force for ordering the world's ills. There is a genuine case to be made that there are governments that are so bad that their disappearance will be a net gain for the world. But this can never justify the global danger of creating a world power that basically is not interested in a world it does not understand, but is capable of intervening by armed force decisively whenever anybody does anything Washington does not like.

Against this background we can see the increasing pressure on the media, because in a world where public opinion is so important, it is also hugely manipulated. Attempts were made during the 1990–1 Gulf War systematically to avoid the Vietnam situation by not letting the media near the action anywhere. But these did not work because there were media, such as CNN, actually in Baghdad, reporting things that did not fit the story as Washington wanted it told. During the Iraq War, control again did not work, so the tendency will be to find yet more effective ways. This may take the form of direct control, maybe even the last resort of technological control, but the combination of governments and monopoly proprietors will be used to even greater effect than with, say, Fox News, or in Italy with Silvio Berlusconi.

How long the present superiority of the Americans will last is impossible to say. The only thing we can be absolutely certain of is that it will be historically a temporary phenomenon, as all other empires have been. In the course of one lifetime we have seen the end of all the colonial empires, the end of the so-called 'Thousand Year Empire' of the Germans (which lasted a mere twelve years), and the end of the Soviet Union's dream of world revolution.

There are internal reasons why the American empire may not last, the most immediate of which is that most Americans are not interested in imperialism or in world domination in the sense of running the world. What they are interested in is what happens to them in the US. The weakness of the US economy is such that at some stage both the US government and electors may decide it's much more important to concentrate on that than to carry on with foreign military adventures; all the more so as in this instance these foreign military interventions will have to be largely paid for by Americans themselves, which was not the case with the Gulf War, nor to a very great extent with the Cold War.

Since 1997–8 we have been living in a crisis of the capitalist world economy. It is not going to collapse, but nevertheless, it is unlikely that the US will continue with ambitious foreign affairs when it has serious problems at home. Even by local business standards Bush does not have an adequate economic policy for the US. And the existing international Bush policy is not a particularly rational one, not for US imperial interests, not for global interests, and certainly not for the interests of US capitalism. Hence the divisions of opinion within the US government.

The key issue now is what the Americans do next, and how other countries will react. Will some countries, such as Britain – the only genuine other member of the ruling coalition – go ahead and back anything the US plans? Essentially, these governments must indicate that there are limits to what the Americans can do with their power. The most positive contribution so far has been made by the Turks, simply by saying there are things they are not prepared to do, even though they know they will pay. But at the moment the major preoccupation is that of, if not containing, at any rate educating, or re-educating, the US. There was a time when the American empire recognised limitations, or at least the desirability of behaving as though it had its limitations. That was largely because they were afraid of somebody else – the Soviet Union. In the absence of this kind of fear, enlightened self-interest and education have to take over.

Notes

1 War and Peace in the Twentieth Century

1 Estimate from Z. Brzezinski, *Out of Control: Global Turmoil on the Eve of the 21st Century* (New York, 1993); population estimate from Angus Maddison, *The World Economy: A Millennial Perspective* (OECD, Paris, 2001), p. 241.

2 See StiftungEntwicklung und Frieden, *Globale Trends 2000: Fakten, Analysen, Prognosen* (Frankfurt a/M, 1999), p. 420, Schaubild 1.

3 Data from UNHCR, *The State of the World's Refugees 2000: Fifty Years of Humanitarian Action* (Oxford, 2000).

4 The best guide to these is Roy Gutman and David Rieff (eds), *Crimes of War: What the Public Should Know* (New York and London, 1999).

2 War, Peace and Hegemony at the Beginning of the Twenty-First Century

1 Paul Bairoch, *De Jéricho à Mexico: Villes et économies dans l'histoire* (Paris, 1985), p. 634.

169

2   Patrick Radden Keefe, 'Iraq, America's Private Armies' in *New York Review of Books*, 12 August 2004, pp. 48–50.
3   *Daily Mail* (London), 22 November 2004, p. 19.
4   Margareta Sollenberg (ed.), *States in Armed Conflict 2000* (Uppsala, 2001); *Internal Displacement: A Global Overview of Trends and Developments in 2003* (http://www.idpproject.org/global_overview.htm).
5   John Steinbrunner and Nancy Gallagher, 'An Alternative Vision of Global Security' in *Daedalus*, summer 2004, p. 84.
6   Angus Maddison, *L'Économie Mondiale 1820–1992. Analyse et Statistiques* (OECD, Paris, 1995), pp. 20–1. The figures for Egypt only from 1900.

3 Why American Hegemony Differs from Britain's Empire

1   Niall Ferguson, *Colossus: The Rise and Fall of the American Empire* (London, 2005).
2   Uppsala, *Uppsala Conflict Data Project (Armed Conflicts 1945–2004)* at prio.no/cwp/ArmedConflict. Consulted 17 June 2006.
3   UNHCR, *The State of the World's Refugees: Human Displacement in the New Millennium* (Oxford 2006), cap. 7, fig. 7.1.
4   Ferguson, op. cit., p. xxviii.
5   *TLS* (London), 29 July 2005.
6   Ferguson, op. cit., p. 42.
7   Friedrich Katz, *The Secret War in Mexico: Europe, the United States and the Mexican Revolution* (Chicago and London, 1981).
8   Howard F. Cline, *Mexico, Revolution to Evolution* (Oxford, New York and Toronto, 1962), p. 141.
9   Christopher Bayly and Tim Harper, *Forgotten Armies: The Fall of British Asia 1941–1945* (London, 2004).
10 League of Nations, *Industrialisation and Foreign Trade* (Geneva, 1943), p. 13.
11 UNIDO *Research Update No.1* (Vienna, January 2006), table, p. 5.
12 Anne Hollander, *Sex and Suits: The Evolution of Modern Dress* (New York, 1994).

13 Jean-Christophe Dumont and Georges Lemaître, 'Counting Immigrants and Expatriates in OECD Countries: A New Perspective' in *OECD Social Employment and Migration Working Papers No. 25* (OECD, Paris, 2003/2006).

14 F. J. Turner, 'Western State-making in the Revolutionary Era' in *American Historical Review I*, 1 October 1895, pp. 70ff.

15 Henry Nash Smith, *Virgin Land: The American West as Symbol and Myth* (New York, 1957).

16 Eric Foner, *The Story of American Freedom* (London, Basingstoke and Oxford, 1998), p. 38.

17 Hannah Arendt, *On Revolution* (New York and London, 1963).

18 Gwyn A. Williams, *Madoc: The Making of a Myth* (Oxford, 1987).

19 Angus Maddison, *L'Économie Mondiale 1820–1992. Analyse et Statistiques* (OECD, Paris, 1995), table 3.3.

20 Calculated from Herbert Feis, *Europe, The World's Banker 1870–1914* (New Haven and London, 1930), p. 23, and Cleona Lewis, *America's Stake in International Investments* (Washington DC, 1938), app. D, p. 606. The \$:£ exchange rate has been roughly estimated at 4.5:1.

21 Eric J. Hobsbawm, with Christopher Wrigley, *Industry and Empire* (London, 1999, new edition), table n32a.

22 Dr F.X. von Neumann-Spallart, *Uebersichten der Weltwirthschaft von Dr F.X. von Neumann-Spallart Jahrgang 1883–84* (Stuttgart, 1887), pp. 189, 226–7, 352–3, 364–6.

23 Angus Maddison, *The World Economy: A Millennial Perspective* (OECD Development Centre, Paris, 2001), app. F 5.

24 W. W. Rostow, *The World Economy: History and Prospect* (London and Basingstoke, 1978), pp. 72–3, 75.

25 *The Economist, Pocket World in Figures* 2004 edition (London, 2003), p. 32.

26 Victoria de Grazia, *Irresistible Empire: America's Advance through Twentieth-Century Europe* (Cambridge, Mass., and London, 2005), p. 213.

27 United Nations Program for Development, *World Report on Human Development* (Brussels, 1999), table 11.

28 Jeffry A. Frieden, *Global Capitalism* (New York and London, 2006), pp. 132, 381.

29   De Grazia, op. cit., p. 1.
30   Frieden, op. cit., p. 133.
31   E.D. Hirsch Jr, Joseph F. Kett and James Trefil, *The New Dictionary of Cultural Literacy* (Boston and New York, 2002).

4 On the End of Empires

1   Jan Morris, 'Islam's Lost Grandeur' in the *Guardian*, 18 September 2004, p. 9 – a review of Mark Mazower, *Salonica, City of Ghosts: Christians, Muslims and Jews 1430–1950* (London, 2004).

5 Nations and Nationalism in the New Century

1   Notably Ernest Gellner, *Nations and Nationalism* (Oxford, 1983); Benedict Anderson, *Imagined Communities: Reflexions on the Origins and Spread of Nationalism* (London, 1983); and A.D. Smith, *Theories of Nationalism* (London, 1983). See also Eric Hobsbawm, *Nations and Nationalism Since 1780* (Cambridge, 1990).
2   Angus Maddison, *The World Economy: A Millennial Perspective* (OECD Development Centre, Paris, 2001), p. 128.
3   *El Pais*, 13 January 2004, p. 11.
4   *Stalker's Guide to International Migration*, table 5, 'Developing Country Remittance Receivers' (2001); (http://pstalker.com/ migration/mg_stats_5.htm).
5   (http://money.cnn.com/2004/10/08/real_estate/mil_life/twopassports/).
6   Benedict Anderson, *The Spectre of Comparisons: Nationalism, Southeast Asia and the World* (London and New York, 1998), pp. 69–71.
7   Pierre Brochand, 'Economie, diplomatie et football' in Pascal Boniface (ed.), *Géopolitique du Football* (Brussels, 1998), p. 78.
8   University of Leicester, Centre for the Sociology of Sport, Fact Sheet 16: *The Bosman Ruling: Football Transfers and Foreign Footballers* (Leicester, 2002).
9   cf. David Goldblatt, *The Ball Is Round: A Global History of Football* (London, 2006), pp. 777–9. See also 'Futbol, Futebol, Soccer:

Football in the Americas', Institute of Latin American Studies Conference, 30–31 October 2003, London (http://www.sas.ac. uk/ilas/sem_football.htm).

10   Eric Hobsbawm, *Nations and Nationalism* (Canto edition), p. 142.

6 The Prospects of Democracy

1   John Dunn, *The Cunning of Unreason: Making Sense of Politics* (London, 2000), p. 210.

2   Herbert Tingsten, *Political Behaviour: Studies in Election Statistics* (London, 1937), pp. 225–6; Seymour Martin Lipset, *Political Man: The Social Bases of Politics* (paperback edition New York, 1963), pp. 227–9.

3   *Prospect*, August–September 1999, p. 57.

4   International Herald Tribune, 2 October 2000, p. 13.

5   ibid.

8 Terror

1   I follow the account in Lawrence Wright, *The Looming Tower* (London, 2006), pp. 123–5, 174–5.

2   Carlos Ivan Degregori et al., *Tiempos de Ira y Amor: Nuevos actores para viejos problemas* (Lima, 1990) is excellent on the 'shining path' (Sendero Luminoso) phenomenon.

3   Martin Pollack, *The Dead Man in the Bunker* (London, 2006), on the life and career of a prominent SS officer.

4   Juan Carlos Marín, *Los Hechos Armados: Argentina 1973–76* (Buenos Aires, 1996), p. 106, cuadro 8.

5   I follow the argument of Diego Gambetta, based on the material in Gambetta (ed.), *Making Sense of Suicide Missions* (Oxford, 2005).

6   Gambetta, op. cit., p. 260.

7   Gambetta, op. cit., p. 270.

8   Wright, op. cit, p. 301.

9   Gambetta, op. cit., p. 327–8.

9 Public Order in an Age of Violence

1   Online Etymological Dictionary.
2   Eric Monkkonen, 'Explaining American Exceptionalism' in *American Historical Review III*, No. 1, February 2006.
3   Danielle Tartakowsky, *Le pouvoir est dans la rue: Crises politiques et manifestations en France* (Paris, 1998), 'Conclusion', especially p. 228.
4   Moisés Naím, *Illicit* (New York, 2005).
5   Chris E. McGooey, 'Gated Communities: Access Control Issues' (www.crimedoctor.com/gated.htm).

Index